# The Right Sticks

## Equipment Myths That Could Wreck Your Golf Game

**Tom Wishon**
with Tom Grundner

SMG
SPORTS
MEDIA
GROUP

SPORTS
MEDIA
GROUP®

All inquiries should be addressed to:
Sports Media Group
An imprint of Ann Arbor Media Group
2500 S. State Street
Ann Arbor, MI 48104

Printed in the United States of America.

1  2  3  4  5  6  7  8  9  10

Library of Congress Cataloging-in-Publication Data

Wishon, Tom W.
  The right sticks : equipment myths that could wreck your golf game / by Tom Wishon with Tom Grundner.
     p. cm.
  ISBN-13: 978-1-58726-498-6 (hardcover : alk. paper)
  ISBN-10: 1-58726-498-6 (hardcover : alk. paper) 1. Golf. 2. Golf--Equipment and supplies. I. Grundner, Thomas. II. Title.

GV965.W738 2008
796.334'2--dc22

                                                    2008000886

# Contents

# Introduction

At some point in your life you have probably played baseball or softball, or maybe played some tennis. All of these are what we call "stick-and-ball" sports, just like golf.

But let me ask you something. When you headed out to buy a bat or racket, what did you see in the sporting goods store?

My guess is that in the bat department, you had a world of options from which to choose. The reason is that every sports equipment dealer commonly stocks bats in different lengths, weights, and handle diameters for each brand and model of bat. They do it that way because both the bat makers and the retailers know that baseball or softball players cannot possibly hit the ball to the best of their ability with bats that all weigh the same, have the same length, the same handle diameter, and so forth.

If you wandered over to the tennis department, you probably saw the premium brands and models of rackets displayed with no strings installed and in a variety of different grip diameters. Here again, the racket makers and sellers know that tennis players cannot play to the best of their ability with rackets of the same grip size, the same string type, and the same string tension. Tennis players choose a grip size to match the size of their hands, and they select the type and tension of the strings to correspond to their swing, power, and manner of play.

Now, think back to your last trip to a golf store. What did you see?

My guess is that you saw row after row of golf clubs. What you probably didn't realize is that all these golf clubs are made to a preordained list of standard specifications: the same length, same weight, same grip size, same everything. If there was a departure from this norm, it was (maybe) a choice of a couple flexes and a couple of lofts—but only in the driver.

Retail golf companies use this standard off-the-rack, one-size-fits-all approach to selling golf clubs for a very good reason: *because they can't (or won't) do it any other way.*

In baseball, softball, tennis, or any other stick-and-ball sport, the games require the player to use only one stick. In golf you use fourteen. Clubmaking companies and their retailers believe they would go out of business if they had to offer sets of golf clubs in all the possible combinations of lengths, weights, grip sizes, and other important custom fitting parameters. They believe the production and inventory management necessary to do that would be nigh on impossible to achieve, so golfers buy standard clubs off-the-rack, while players in the other sports get to choose a custom piece of equipment, matched far better to their size, strength, athletic ability, and swing skills.

The problem is that this is the way most golfers believe it is *supposed* to be. That it somehow *has* to be that way. Of all the stick-and-ball sports, golfers are somehow expected to play with clubs of the same length, the same lie angles, same face angles, same weight, and so on through all the various parameters that make a golf club what it is.

But it doesn't have to be that way. In fact, nothing could be further from the truth.

Throughout this book I will continually harp on one central theme, and it is this: *The best golf clubs you will ever have are those that are custom tailored to your individual size, strength, athletic ability, and swing characteristics.* I know that's not what you're used to hearing, and it is certainly *not* what the major club companies and golf stores want you to hear. But a lifetime in the golf club design industry has taught me this—it's the absolute truth.

To the club companies and retail stores, however, things can never be that way because of the calculus of retail sales. Fourteen clubs times a variety of fitting parameters, times several options within each fitting parameter adds up, to them, to an impossible number of units to make and stock. But do you see what's happening? They have made *their* problem into *your* problem—and worse, they have you convinced that that's just fine!

Let me ask you a simple question. Would you buy a $400 suit of clothes without having needed adjustments made? Would you even shop at a clothing store that didn't at least have access to a qualified tailor? If not, then could you please tell me why on earth you would buy a $1,500 set of golf clubs without demanding the same thing that you would with a $400 suit?

Two problems are feeding this situation. The first will occupy the bulk of this book, and the second I will cover in the final chapter.

To begin with, people want clothes that fit correctly because they know how correctly fitted clothes are supposed to look and feel. Most golfers have no such frame of reference for their golf clubs. The average golfer knows little more about golf clubs than what they see in golf magazine advertising or on Golf Channel infomercials. As a result, they have bought into a lot of myths about golf equipment that keep them from being all that they could be as golfers. I hope to dispel at least some of those myths in this book.

The second problem, however, is more complex. Retail clothing stores have qualified tailors at hand because they know their customers expect it. Retail golf stores do *not* have qualified custom clubmakers at hand because golfers have been trained to *not* expect it. It's as simple as that, and it's something I hope to see changed. That's why the last chapter of this book was written.

You see, tailored, professionally custom fitted golf clubs are NOT only for really good golfers, and they are NOT more expensive than the "one-size-fits-all" clubs you buy off the rack in the big retail stores. In fact, if anything, the less skilled you are as a golfer, the *more* you need clubs that are tailored to your size, your strength, your athletic ability, and your individual swing characteristics.

At this point, however, to be fitted with clubs like these, you will need to go to a skilled, experienced, independent custom clubmaker, and that's something the golf industry does not want you to hear. With a custom clubmaker "national averages" go out the window. It's one club, one customer, one clubmaker. It is drilled into the professional clubmaker's head from day one that there is no such thing as gender or age when it comes to fitting golfers. There are only golfers with differences in their size, strength, athletic ability, and swing characteristics. What's more, you will rarely, if ever, pay more than what you would have paid for equivalent clubs bought off the rack.

To the average golfer, that philosophy can make all the difference in the world.

There is one more point I would like to emphasize—and for me it is important that you understand it.

Except for a few years directly after college when I began my career in golf as a PGA club pro, I have spent my entire working life in the field of golf club design and custom clubfitting research. I have designed for several different well-known golf club brand names and have more than fifty design "firsts" to my name. I've designed club models that have been used to win on the PGA Tour, on the Champions Tour, and in Ryder Cup competition. A few years ago I was offered a job as the chief designer for a huge national firm. I turned it down, and instead started my own golf club design and clubmaking supply company called Tom Wishon Golf Technology.

Now, you might read that and ask: "Aren't you therefore writing these books because you simply want to sell your golf club designs?" The answer is no, because at the age of fifty-seven with thirty-five years in the golf business, it's not about six-figure salaries and selling hundreds of thousands of golf clubs. To me, it's about educating golfers that there is a better way out there to obtain golf clubs that will allow you to play a little better and enjoy this great game a little more. I've seen countless golfers improve their shotmaking and their handicaps, and thus increase the level of enjoyment in the game, once they began to work with a good, knowledgeable custom clubmaker. And that brings me to the point I want you to understand.

*I am not saying the things I do because I am in the custom clubfitting side of the golf equipment business. I am in the custom clubfitting side of the golf equipment business because I believe the things I am saying!*

Since I was about twelve years old, golf has been my passion. There have literally been thousands of days on which I have thanked my father, who, without even asking me, signed me up for golf lessons when I was a kid. I dearly love the game.

But when I see other golfers, who also love the game, being fooled—when I see the game being potentially harmed by the kind of equipment-induced frustration that in some cases is actually driving people away from the sport—then I *have* to do something about it. And, right now, that's what I see happening.

Each year about the same number of people leave the game of golf as start playing. Statistics say the average golfer's handicap is 17, the same it was thirty years ago before all of this high-tech, over-engineered golf equipment began to show up in pro shops and off-course golf stores. When they are surveyed, one of the major reasons given by those who give up golf is "frustration with the game." Now, I'll be the first to admit that golf can be a frustrating game even for the best players. But how much of this frustration is due to what I call the "grass ceiling"? By that I mean the ongoing public embarrassment of poor performance caused by golf equipment that not only will not—*but cannot possibly*—meet the golfer's needs.

If you don't believe that such frustration exists, go to any driving range on a busy day and watch for a while. People of all shapes and sizes, of every gender and age, with good swings, bad swings, and everything in between, will be at the tee line flailing away. A few shots will be excellent, some indifferent; many of them will be bad, and some downright dangerous to surrounding life, limb, and property.

Watch especially when these golfers take out their drivers. If you see two or three golfers out of ten who can consistently hit the ball straight and on a nice trajectory, you're there on a good day. I am not talking about hitting 300-yard drives down the middle. I am talking about the ball flying high and relatively straight, landing downrange at any reasonable distance, within 20 or 30 yards on either side of its intended target.

Now, think about what you're seeing.

Name one other product that, in the hands of the average consumer, is so demandingly difficult to use that it works properly only two or three times out of ten. In any other industry it would be a scandal, and companies would be going out of business overnight—but not in the golf industry. In the world of golf, we give each other knowing winks and say, in tones of sympathetic camaraderie, "It's a hell of a tough game, isn't it?"

But that feeling of "sympathetic camaraderie" does not usually last very long. Many people finally walk off the golf course and vow they will never again be humiliated like that in front of other people. Or they just begin to lose interest in a game that brings more frustration than enjoyment.

That's the harm that's being done. But it's also, given my professional knowledge and experience, something that I am well qualified to do something about—and after thirty-five years of watching this happen to golfers, I have vowed to do just that.

Many of you might remember a story from your childhood. It's the one where two con men convince the king that they could make him a suit of clothes from a cloth so fine it was invisible to anyone who was stupid. All the learned men of the realm praised the king's clothes, of course, because they didn't want to appear stupid. This lasted until a small child finally cried out, "But the king has no clothes on!" And the fraud came undone.

I guess in many ways that's what this book is about. It is saying, if no one else will, that if you look closely the king really *is* without clothes. But it would be hypocritical for me to stop there. In the last chapter I point out what each group within the golf industry needs to do to help eliminate the grass ceiling. And, yes, included on that list is my own company and you, the average golfer.

It is to the goal of making the game of golf more fun, for more people, that this book is dedicated. So let's start the process by covering more than three dozen myths—false beliefs that many golfers have about golf equipment—and try shedding some light on each one.

Enjoy and learn!

Tom Wishon
Durango, CO

# Clubheads

# Myth #1

# Modern golf clubs hit the ball farther than the older ones.

If you are like most golfers, you're concerned with how far you can hit the ball off the tee. After a few hours of watching the Golf Channel or paging through almost any golf magazine, it's easy for you to become convinced that your old standbys need to be set aside for a new and "longer-hitting" set. The problem is that most of the newer clubs really do not hit farther than the older ones. What you are seeing is basically a marketing and sales gimmick.

Let's begin at the beginning.

Three things primarily determine the distance you hit a golf ball: the mass of the clubhead, its loft, and the speed at which the head impacts the ball. Okay? That's Physics 101, and even the golf gods do not have the power to suspend the laws of physics.

But there is a dark side to that formula, and it is this: *the longer the length, the lower the loft, the heavier the weight, and the stiffer the shaft—the harder the club will be to hit.*

Over the past few years your body's swing speed has probably stayed about the same, but unfortunately your clubs have not. This is due to something I call the "vanishing loft disease."

Starting about twenty-five years ago, in order to be able to say their clubs "hit farther," the makers of both men and women's clubs have been tinkering with the loft angles of their clubheads—lowering them a bit at a time without telling you. As a result, by now every club in the set has moved up at least one, if not two, numbers.

The club companies realized that 99 percent of all golfers know their clubs only by the number on the sole and not by how many degrees of loft were designed into each. To most golfers, a 5-iron is a 5-iron, right? So imagine the legions of thrilled golfers who picked up the 5-iron from a shiny new set and found they could hit it 10 or 20 yards farther than their old one. That's hardly surprising, of course, because that shiny new 5-iron in their hands was a 4-iron only a few years before, and probably a 3-iron a few years before that. But were you told that was happening, or did the magazine and TV ads just say something about "new and improved technology"?

If you somehow think this vanishing loft phenomenon is not happening, take a look at the numbers in the table below.

As an extra benefit (to the club companies), this vanishing loft disease has forced golfers to buy additional clubs that they

### The Dreaded Vanishing Loft Disease

Evolution of Men's Wood & Iron Lofts—Industry Average

| Club | 1960s–70s (degrees) | 1980s (degrees) | Early 1990s (degrees) | 1997+ (degrees) |
|------|------|------|------|------|
| 1-iron | 17 | 17 | 16 | 16–17 |
| 2-iron | 20 | 20 | 19 | 18–20 |
| 3-iron | 24 | 23 | 22 | 20–21 |
| 4-iron | 28 | 26 | 25 | 23–24 |
| 5-iron | 32 | 30 | 28 | 26–27 |
| 6-iron | 36 | 34 | 32 | 30–31 |
| 7-iron | 40 | 38 | 36 | 34–35 |
| 8-iron | 44 | 42 | 40 | 38–40 |
| 9-iron | 48 | 46 | 44 | 42–44 |
| PW | 52 | 50 | 48 | 46–48 |
| SW | 56 | 56 | 56 | 55–56 |
| Driver | 11 | 11 | 10 | 9–10.5 |
| 3-wood | 16 | 15 | 15 | 13–14 |
| 5-wood | 22 | 21 | 19 | 17–18 |
| 7-wood | 28 | 27 | 23 | 20–21 |

*Note:* A quick look at the information above shows how drastically golf club companies have reduced their loft angles over the past few decades. This was done primarily so they could say their clubs hit the ball farther and thereby sell more clubs. Unfortunately, it also makes the clubs much harder to hit.

otherwise would not have needed. Again, let's start with some background.

In the world of clubfitting there is something called the "24/38 Rule." Basically, it says that the average golfer—male or female, young or old—cannot even come close to consistently hitting an iron that has less than 24 degrees of loft or is more than 38 inches in length. The reason is that a club like that requires a swing precision that most amateurs don't have the time or the ability to acquire.

A few years ago the 24/38 line fell to the far side of the 3-iron. So, when you bought a set of clubs, you bought a 3-iron through a pitching wedge, and you could reasonably expect to hit each of those clubs. Because of the vanishing loft disease, however, the 24/38 line has now moved past the territory of the 5-iron—making the 3-, 4- and now even the 5-iron *un*hittable for most people.

So, what are you supposed to do? It's simple. The club companies want you *to buy three or four more clubs* to compensate for the corner that *they* painted you into.

You are now supposed to buy something called "hybrid" clubs, which are easy-to-hit substitutes for the 3-, 4- and 5-irons that are no longer usable by the majority of golfers. In addition, as all the irons have now moved up and away from the sand wedge, you are now supposed to buy something called a "gap wedge" to fill in the "gap" *they* created with their loft-shrinking marketing stunts.

Terrific.

# Myth #2

# The lower the loft on your driver, the farther the ball will go.

Yup, that's true … with your fairway woods, hybrids, and your irons. But—pick your pro tour circuit—even with the swing speed of a Tiger Woods, Karin Sjodin, or Craig Stadler, there is a point at which the driver loft will be too low even for golfers like that to generate their longest driving distances. Sure, for them that loft number might be a single digit, but the rest of us mere mortals need a *higher* loft to get more distance, one that is definitely double-digit, and for many golfers is probably a number with a "teen" after it.

I know that sounds counterintuitive, so I'll explain it this way.

I am sure that at one time or another you've played around with a garden hose. Imagine you have the hose turned on full blast, and you're trying to get as much distance as possible out of the water spray. Now, suppose someone turns the water pressure back by about a third. You can feel the pressure drop in your hands and see the loss of distance in the spray. So, what do you automatically do to try to get some of that distance back? Exactly! You raise the angle of the nozzle.

It's the same way with the driver.

If you're among the relatively few golfers who have a very high swing speed (i.e., the hose is on full blast), you need a lower loft to get maximum distance. If, like most golfers, you have a slower swing speed (i.e., the hose pressure has been cut back), you need a *higher* loft to get more distance. *What you cannot do is match a low swing speed with a low-lofted driver!* That's the equivalent of lowering the water pressure *and* lowering the nozzle angle, and wondering why the water isn't going as far.

So, how fast can you reasonably expect to swing your driver *with control?* Here are some numbers that might give you a sense of where you probably fall. I've listed some average driver swing speeds, and I've also included a chart that shows the average carry distance (before the roll of the ball) with drivers of different loft. It's easy to see the difference a higher loft makes.

Average Woman Golfer: 65 mph
Average Male Golfer: 87 mph

Average Woman Tour Player: 97 mph
Average Male Tour Player: 113 mph

Female Long-Drive Competitors: 105–120 mph
Male Long-Drive Competitors: 135–155 mph

### Carry Distance in Yards before Roll

| Swing Speed (mph) | Driver Loft 9° | Driver Loft 11° | Driver Loft 13° | Driver Loft 15° | Driver Loft 17° |
|---|---|---|---|---|---|
| 50 | 57 | 65 | 72 | 77 | **81** |
| 60 | 91 | 102 | 109 | 115 | **119** |
| 70 | 131 | 142 | 149 | 153 | **156** |
| 80 | 170 | 179 | 184 | **186** | 185 |
| 90 | 205 | 211 | **213** | 212 | 211 |
| 100 | 234 | **237** | 236 | 234 | 230 |
| 110 | **258** | 257 | 254 | 249 | 243 |
| 120 | **277** | 274 | 268 | 261 | 253 |

*Note:* The carry distances shown here are calculated assuming a level angle of attack into the ball.

In the above chart I have boldfaced and underlined the driver loft where you will get maximum distance at each swing speed. Notice anything strange?

You will not achieve maximum carry distance with any loft lower than 15 degrees until your swing speed *with control* gets at or near 90 mph. Now, I ask you: when was the last time you walked into a golf retail store and saw a driver with 17 degrees of loft, or 15 degrees? How about 13 degrees? May we then assume that all of you have swing speeds *with control* of 100-plus mph—a speed greater than the average LPGA Tour player and only a bit less than the average PGA Tour pro?

Are you getting the picture here?

Have you ever wondered why you sometimes hit your 3-wood or even your 5-wood farther than you hit your driver? Now you know why.

Think about that the next time you walk into your next twenty-thousand-square-foot, big-box retail golf store and see row after row of 9- and 10-degree drivers on the rack.

You think those clubs were designed for *you?*

# Myth #3
# The harder the clubface, or the higher the strength of its material, the more distance you will get.

Can we get it out of our heads that because your clubhead is made out of a high-strength or ultra-hard material, it will hit the ball farther?

At one point or another, drivers have been made from nearly everything—wood, steel, plastic, aluminum, graphite, titanium, and even ceramics. Shortly after "wooden woods" were replaced by steel in the early 1980s, the marketing experts decided they had free rein to tout almost any non-wooden, super-hard or super-strong material as the next greatest golf club. If the material was harder than wood, it had to hit the ball farther, right? Well, the answer is no.

Do you remember, under Myth #1, where I said the primary factors that affect the distance you hit a golf ball are the mass of the clubhead, its loft, and the speed at which the head impacts the ball? That was not technobabble, folks. It's basic physics. Besides those factors the only other thing that matters is the strength and elasticity of the face material and how those affect the ability of the face to flex when you hit the ball (without having it break or cave in).

The reason the vast majority of drivers today are made from some variety of titanium is that titanium has "the right stuff" from a manufacturing standpoint. What I mean is that it has the right combination of lightness, strength, and elasticity so that your driver head can approach the size of a grapefruit and still weigh the right amount, so that it will not collapse like a cheap tent when hit, and so that it will still fall within the United States Golf Association's (USGA) limit for spring face capability, officially known as the COR Rule (see Myth #4).

Prior to the use of titanium as a driver face material, it didn't matter if the face of your driver was made from a block of wood, a block of steel, or a block of granite. The energy transfer from the clubhead to the ball was about the same, so there were no real differences in shot distance.

When titanium came on the market, the fact that the metal possessed greater elasticity than any other driver head material meant that some incredibly wild claims could accompany its entry into millions of golfers' bags. But clubhead hardness has *nothing* to do with how far the ball will travel. It might affect how easily your club gets banged up in the bag, but distance? No way.

No super high-strength metal will be allowed to exceed the USGA's COR Rule—no matter how strong that metal may be. As long as the club companies follow that USGA rule, your shot distance will be primarily determined by how well you are custom fitted for length, loft, shaft weight, shaft flex, and swingweight.

That's Physics 101, not Marketing 399.

As far as hardness and strength affecting your ability to work the ball flight—again, there is no way. Workability (the ability to intentionally fade or draw the ball) is all about the club's *design.* How is the weight distributed? Where is the center of gravity? What is its moment of inertia? These have nothing to do with the type of metal being used.

You might want to also keep in mind that in the 1960s Jack Nicklaus won a long drive competition against his fellow PGA Tour players with a 343-yard shot—using a persimmon wood driver of 42¾-inch length with a steel shaft.

Now, I am not saying you should go out and buy a persimmon driver—unless your name happens to be Jack Nicklaus (in which case Mr. Nicklaus, sir, you can hit anything you want). What I am saying is that titanium is indeed better for drivers, but it's not because it is "harder." What titanium brings to the party is a combination of face elasticity and overall strength. *That's* what makes it better.

I know whereof I speak. In the twenty-one years I have been a golf club designer, I have designed something north of one hundred different driver head models using everything from aluminum to zinc, and there is no question that the strength-to-elasticity relationship of titanium makes it the best driver face material for achieving your potential for distance.

However, whether you achieve your full potential for distance depends less on the material from which the face is made, and far more on whether you get the right driver length, loft, face angle, shaft, swingweight, and grip size, to match your size, strength, athletic ability, and swing.

# Myth #4
# The bigger the head (or the stranger its shape), the better a driver will perform.

Sometimes I think there isn't an easier task in all of marketing than to convince people that "bigger is better," regardless of whether we're talking about cars or cheeseburgers. If you follow golf at all, you're well aware that big head shapes are very "in" these days and "driver envy" is now measured in cubic centimeters.

In more than thirty years as a clubhead designer, I've never seen a trend move from drawing board to commonplace faster than the development of driver heads designed to push the USGA's maximum allowed volume/size of 470cc.[1] I guess the fact that it is now almost impossible to find a driver smaller than that is the best testimony I can offer for how compelling "bigger is better" marketing can be.

There are two performance related factors that can be improved when a clubhead is made larger in size and volume. In terms of today's 460cc jumbo-size driver heads, however, one of these factors is limited by USGA rules, while the other is probably already doing about as much as it's going to do for you with your current club.

Let's take them one at a time.

The first supposed advantage is that the bigger the driver head, the larger the face can be made. And the larger the face area,

---

[1] For you equipment and rule hawks, I know the USGA says the limit is 460cc; but it allows a tolerance of 10cc, so the driver head limit is really 470cc.

the more potential exists for increasing the spring-like effect of the face. The problem is, in 1998 the USGA decided they'd had enough of driver heads with ever-increasing "spring" (known as the Coefficient of Restitution or COR), so they clamped a pair of very rigid handcuffs on all of us designers.

This came in the form of the 0.830 COR limit on the faces of clubheads. (In other words, if you shoot a golf ball at a driver head at 100 mph, it better not come back faster than 83 mph.) As a result, while a bigger face could theoretically enable us to provide you with a hotter driver, we can't do that, or else that driver will be labeled as non-conforming to the USGA Rules of Golf. And that, my friends, removes the larger face from being an advantage on the new larger heads.

But that still leaves us with the other "bigger is better" performance issue: namely, the idea that the bigger the head, the more forgiving it will be for off-center hits.

There is absolutely no question that an off-center hit from one of today's 460cc grapefruits will take off with a smidge more ball velocity than the same shot with a 350cc or smaller driver head. So, if you're currently using a sub-350cc club and you suffer from occasional-to-frequent off-center hits, moving to a 460cc head might be something of an improvement.

On the other hand, if you have already bought one of the three or four million 460cc oversized driver heads that have been produced and sold in the last few years, you've probably already gotten about as much shot-forgiveness as you're going to get. Buying yet another club—be it round, square, or triangular—will not help any. But to explain why, we have to head over for another brief visit to Physics 101.

Every object has a center of gravity, which is the intersection of all the possible balance points of that object. If you remove the driver head from the shaft and your hands are steady, you can balance it on top of a pencil eraser. You can do it on the head's face, on its sole, on its top, or on almost any of its surfaces. Inside the head, there will be one point at which all those balance points intersect. That's the center of gravity (CG) of the head.

When we golfers make contact with the ball out toward the toe or heel of the face, the head will respond by trying to rotate around the CG. The higher the moment of inertia (MOI, or resistance to twisting) the head has, the less it will twist in response to an off-center hit. The lower the MOI, the more the head will twist. The more the head twists, the more energy it loses, and the more distance is lost … but *only* for off-center hits. On-center hit performance is still controlled by the COR, for which, as I explained above, there is a limit in the rules. When you hit the ball on-center with the driver, there is no head rotation about the CG axis, and the MOI of the head has no function in shot performance whatsoever.

All right, so what about those square- or triangular-shaped drivers that profess to have a higher MOI? Well, actually, they *do* have a higher MOI, but I'm going to let you in on a little industrial secret. It's one that any scientifically knowledgeable club designer will tell you … as long as his right hand is on a Bible, you've bought him a beer, and no one from his company's marketing department is anywhere nearby.

For most people, it's not a difference that's going to make a difference. Here's why.

Moment of inertia can be measured with a very sophisticated piece of equipment that gives us the MOI measurement of a head in "grams centimeter squared." I know, that's Physics 201, and I am not going to make you suffer through that, but bear with me here.

Most conventionally shaped 460cc drivers have an MOI in a range between 4200 and 4700 g-cm$^2$. Some of the square- or triangular-shaped drivers are claiming an MOI between 5,000 and 5,250 g-cm$^2$. So the question you need to have answered before you load your credit card with a $400–$500 charge is, *how much game improvement am I going to get for those additional 550 to 1,000 MOI points?*

The answer for most of you is: little or none.

If you're currently playing with a smaller-size driver that has been accurately fitted for length, loft, face angle, shaft, swing-weight, and grip size, then you might see a *smidge* of distance improvement with off-center hits. The operative word here being "smidge."

On the other hand, if you're still playing with a driver you bought straight off the rack, and you've had nothing altered on that driver to better fit your game ... then fuhgettabout the MOI. It's the least of your problems. A club that is not fitted properly will instantly and totally overwhelm any small performance advantage those 550 to 1,000 additional MOI points might give you.

Without proper fitting, buying another $400 standard-made, mass-produced driver off the rack just because it has a higher MOI number makes no sense in view of the fact that more than 90 percent of all golfers have never thought about the much greater benefits of being professionally custom fitted for the best length, loft, face angle, shaft, weight, and grip size.

# Myth #5
# Your new driver has a larger sweet spot.

Actually, there are some drivers that really do have a larger "sweet spot," but only if you are prepared to *mis*define that term as a face that doesn't lose as much of its ability to flex inward when an off-center impact occurs.

The problem is, there is no such thing in the golf industry as a "sweet spot-o-meter" that you or anyone else can use to determine which drivers do or do not possess what they claim to possess. Currently, the only "measurement devices" that are used to inform you of a club's "sweetspotted-ness" exist in the ads that attracted your attention in the first place!

"Sweet spot" is a term that's commonly found in those golf club ads, but it's misused by almost everyone. Technically the sweet spot is a point inside the head called the center of gravity that's about the size of the sharp end of a pin. It can't get "larger" and it can't get "smaller." It just … is.

IF you have a club that has the right loft for your swing type and swing speed, and IF it strikes the ball square, and IF it hits the exact center of the golf ball directly in line with this tiny sweet spot—then the ball will fly the greatest possible distance for your particular swing. Any deviation toward the heel or toe from this perfect contact and the head will start to twist, not only imparting a curving flight to the ball, but also causing a loss of distance. The farther your point of contact is from this tiny sweet spot, the more distance and accuracy you lose. To be more specific, depending on how well the designer manipulated the face thickness over its entire area, you will lose at best about 3–4 yards flight distance, and at worst as much as 10 yards, for each half-inch by which you miss the center of the face.

When club companies talk about an "increased sweet spot," what they're really saying is one of two things. First, they've done things in the clubhead's design to increase the *moment of inertia* of the clubhead. In other words, they put weight on the sides and/or in the back of the head to make it twist a little less (with the accent on *little*) when you miss the sweet spot. The second possibility involves what I've been talking about, the design of the face itself.

You already know that a driver face flexes inward when you hit the ball. The more you can flex the face, the higher your ball speed will be when it comes off the face. But here again, if you miss the center when you make contact with the ball, that mishit part of the face can't flex as much; the head vibrates and twists as it loses energy, and you will never achieve your maximum distance. By making the outer edges of the face a little thinner than the center, however, it's possible to make the face flex a little more when you hit the ball off center so you won't lose as much distance. Typically this takes the form of a face that is a little thicker in the center, but then thinner in the areas all around it.

But let's subject all this to a reality check.

There are indeed a few drivers with such well-designed faces that a shot hit as much as one inch off center will only lose 2–3 percent of the distance you can get when you hit the club on center. The other "smaller sweet spot" clubs lose 4 to 5 percent. Sounds good, huh? But let's do some math. Let's see, if you hit a drive 200 yards, the "larger sweet spot" club will give you a gain of approximately a whopping two yards. Two yards! And you want to pay extra for that?!

How about this instead? Since the driver they sold you probably has a longer length than even the pros use on the PGA Tour, and since the longer the length the more you hit the ball off center, why not simply go get fitted for a shorter driver so you don't have to worry about sweet spots and twisting—large, small, or in-between?

And while you're at it, why not really do your game a favor and have the driver fitted for the proper loft, face angle, shaft, weight, and grip size at the same time? Then you'll really discover what the words "game improvement design" mean.

# Myth #6

# You can change the flight of the ball by putting lead tape on your clubhead.

Just about every golf store I've ever gone into has a "stuff display." You know what I mean. These are all the little gadgets and doo-hickeys you can buy for a few bucks to alter or improve your golf game—or, failing that, at least give you something to talk about with your golfing buddies. I don't know about you, but I can't resist giving those stuff displays at least a once-over.

But there is a limit to what I will invest even a few bucks in, and that limit is with stuff I *know* cannot possibly work. Lead tape falls into that category.

It begins one evening when you are peacefully watching a PGA practice round on TV. They zoom the camera into a player's bag, and you see the pro has little strips of lead tape on the back of his clubs. "Eureka!" (or similar expletive) you cry. "So, that's their secret!"

You rush off to your local big box golf store, run to the gadget and "stuff" aisle, and snatch up the object of your desire—a package of lead tape strips. You turn the package over and there it is:

**To hit the ball higher:** Add tape to the back of the club and low.

**To cure a slice:** Put tape toward the heel—it will help the clubface to rotate closed.

**To cure a hook:** Put tape toward the toe—it will help keep the clubface open.

**If your club just doesn't feel right:** Put tape wherever you bloody well feel like, and it will change the swingweight.

So which of those statements is false? Never mind. For the answer I'll just refer you to Mark Twain's observations on common sense—that it's not common at all.

Let's say you buy a package that has half-inch wide tape strips cut into two-inch lengths. Now, for you to notice any difference in your ball flight (i.e., higher, lower, left, or right), the center of gravity of the club will have to be moved at least one-quarter inch through the addition of weight in the various desired locations on the head. The problem as defined by Physics 101 is to determine how much lead tape will that take? Better buy a couple of packages because it will take twenty (!) of those strips, all piled on top of each other on the side of the head opposite to where you want the ball to change flight, before you even *begin* to notice a difference.

But what about the last claim, that you can change the swing-weight of the club by using lead tape? That's true, you can, and that is the one and only truly valuable and fact-based purpose for using lead tape on your clubheads.

We will talk a lot more about swingweight later on, but for now let's just say that swingweight is the perceived heaviness of the head when you grip the club and swing it. Having the right headweight for your individual strength and swing tempo is critical for improving how often you make contact with the ball in the center of the face. As I hope you've learned by now, hitting the ball on center is the number-one way to reach your full distance and accuracy potential.

So if you find yourself thinking that your club heads feel a little too light, slap that lead tape anywhere you want on the head. Feel free to experiment and see if you can find a point where your swing tempo calms down and you start catching the ball more often in the center of the face.

As a rule of thumb, the stronger you are physically and the faster or more forcefully you swing at the ball, the higher the swingweight and headweight of your clubs need to be to help you slow down and drop to a more consistent swing tempo. The clubs you buy off the rack are made to one and only one swingweight. The problem is that golfers do not come in one and only one variety of strength and swing tempo, so this opens up a potentially large area of improvement for some people just by experimenting with a little lead tape.

If you do that and you like the "heavier" feel, great. Now take your club to a professional clubmaker and ask him or her to properly re-swingweight your club to that new weight, unless you don't mind the lead-tape look of your clubheads.

So, why do the pros use lead tape? Well, if you want to talk about a group of golfers who are always hunting for the equipment version of the Holy Grail, you're talking about the guys on the Tour. But there are two things that don't last very long in this world: dogs chasing cars and pros putting for pars.

We're all impressed with the pros' ability to "get it up and down for par." But the pros know that cashing checks (and perpetuating all those freebies showered upon them at every PGA Tour stop) depends on how many times they're putting for birdie. That means hitting more greens in regulation and having more of those shots end up closer to the hole, which comes only from consistent ball striking.

To the pros, consistent ball striking is all about the *feel* of their clubs, and headweight feel, a.k.a. swingweight, plays a huge role. So when you see lead tape all over a pro's clubheads, what you're seeing is them using lead tape for the same reason you might. They are hunting for the right headweight feel, which begets a more consistent swing, which begets more consistent ball flight, which begets more greens hit in regulation, which begets more birdies, which begets more money and free stuff from each tournament's sponsor. And lead tape is the easiest way to begin that hunt.

So if you're just playing with standard clubs you bought off the rack, and you get the feeling you either can't feel the weight of the head or you can't get yourself to "slow down," head to the range with a few packets of lead tape and have at it. Just don't expect that putting lead tape on the heel, toe, sole, or top of the head will have any effect on the direction and height you hit the ball.

# Myth #7

# The second-longest-hitting club in your bag is your 3-wood.

The good news is that you *do* have a second-longest-hitting wood; it's just that it might not be the one with a number 3 engraved in the sole.

Let's start with the concept of the "second-longest-hitting" wood. I am defining that as whatever wood you will primarily use to hit the ball as far as possible off the grass, without the assistance of a tee. Any golfer with a swing speed under 130 mph, who isn't usually going at par-5 holes with an iron on his or her second shot, needs one. In other words, pretty much every golfer needs a "second-longest-hitting wood." So, here's how you find it.

You might have simply assumed your "second" was your 3-wood and not thought much more about it. After all, that's the natural order of the universe, isn't it: driver, 3-wood, 5-wood?

But what happens if we throw out the numbers that are on the bottom of your clubs and go with a functional analysis? If you absorbed the facts of life (in Myth #2) about the loft angle you need on your driver to maximize your distance, you learned two things. First, you know that slower-swing-speed players need higher lofts to get maximum distance. And second, slower-swinging players don't hit the ball as high for any given loft angle.

But let's say you've been professionally custom fitted for a driver loft that maximizes your distance off the tee. In the search for your perfect "second-longest-hitting wood," please don't just automatically grab a wood with the number 3 on the sole.

Why not? Well, for one thing, because not all 3-woods are designed with the same loft.

Do you remember the clubfitting credo I laid on you earlier—the one that says: *the longer the length, the lower the loft, the heavier the weight, and the stiffer the shaft—the harder the club will be to hit?* Well, focus on that second clause, the "lower the loft" part; then keep in mind that when we're talking fairway woods, we're talking about clubs that are not normally used with nice, long, confidence-building tees.

Unfortunately, the same vanishing loft disease that has made today's 3-, 4- and even 5-irons unhittable for most golfers has also made the 3-wood unhittable off the ground for a whole lot of golfers as well!

Thirty years ago, the average 3-wood loft was 16 degrees for men and 17 degrees for women. Today, woods with the number 3 on the sole can be 12, 13, 14, or 15 degrees, and women no longer routinely get that extra degree tacked on. In short, the vast majority of golfers do not have the skill to hit a modern-era 3-wood high enough off the fairway to make it into their second-longest-hitting wood.

If you read Myth #2 you know that the primary purpose of today's off-the-rack driver is to get you to buy one. No one who sells standard-made drivers off the rack actually expects you to be able to hit it consistently well. You now know that if you possess a driver swing speed of 95 mph or lower, you have no business swinging that 9-degree, 46-inch garden tool. And a quick glance at the chart on page 7 tells you that the correct driver loft for the average male golfer's swing speed of 87 mph will be somewhere around 13 or 14 degrees.

Now, let's see: if the correct loft for your driver is 13 or 14 degrees, then your next club down would be 17 or 18 degrees, and the next one after that would be 20 or 21 degrees.

What? You say you just checked the loft on your clubs, and your 3-wood is your "driver," your 5-wood is really your "3-wood," and your 7-wood is really your "5-wood?"

Why … I am shocked!

Well, okay, maybe I am not shocked. In fact, maybe it's time to introduce some data here that might help you find the club that you should actually be using in that long second shot to the green.

| Driver Swing Speed (mph) | Angle of Attack | Best Driver Loft | Carry Distance | Second-Longest Wood Loft |
|:---:|:---:|:---:|:---:|:---:|
| 60 | Level | 17 | 119 | 17–20 |
| 70 | Level | 17 | 156 | 17–20 |
| 80 | Level | 15 | 186 | 15–18 |
| 90 | Level | 13 | 213 | 14–16 |
| 100 | Level | 11 | 237 | 14–16 |

Some golfers, regardless of their swing speed, do have the swing ability to hit a little lower loft well up in the air. If you have no problem getting the ball up off the ground, use the lower figure in the "Second-Longest Wood Loft" column. If you struggle with consistently getting the ball up off the ground, use the higher loft. If you're in between, well then ... pick something in between.

As you can see, if you have a genuine 100 percent All-American 80–90 mph swing speed (with control!), then you're looking at a second-longest club of somewhere in the 14- to 18-degree range. And that, in turn, will place either a higher-lofted 3-wood, or more likely a 5-wood, in your hands for that important second shot.

If you are in the 60–70 mph swing speed range (and many senior and lady golfers are), you are looking at taking your second shot with a high-lofted 5-wood, or more likely a 7-wood.

I did not include data on anyone with a swing speed of 110 mph in the data for a reason—because there are hardly any of you out there.[2] Now, don't get your Y chromosomes in an uproar. I am not saying you don't matter. I am simply trying to make a point.

Throughout this book when I talk about swing speed I am talking about swing speed *with control.* In other words, anyone can swing out of his or her shoes and clock a higher swing speed. My father can do it! And sometimes, when the golf gods are

---

[2] OK, sorry. Since my own swing speed has just dropped a few mph south of 100, maybe I'm into some kind of swing speed denial and there really are more of you out there than I think. For you who really do have a 110 mph driver swing speed, your best loft for maximum carry distance is 9 degrees, and your best bet for the "second-longest-hitting wood" will probably be a 3-wood with 13 to 15 degrees of loft.

occupied tormenting someone else, you might actually hit a ball straight and long with that comin'-outta-your-shoes swing. But that's not what I am talking about here.

Let me put it to you another way. If you made a 10 mph swing, my guess is that you could hit the ball straight every time. If you come out of your shoes to reach a 110 mph swing speed, my guess is (come on, let's be honest) most of the time it's a crap shoot as to where that ball is going. If it lands on the fairway it's as much a surprise to you as it is to anyone. That means that somewhere between 10 and 110 mph *is your swing speed*. It's the speed with which you can land anywhere on the fairway at least 7 out of 10 times. That's the swing speed I am talking about. (And if you don't know where that swing speed is, for the sake of your game, you'd better get to a driving range and find it.)

So, let's put all this in a nutshell. You need a second-longest-hitting club. That club might very well be something other than your 3-wood, because your 3-wood might actually be your driver, and your 5-wood might actually be your 3-wood, unless your 7-wood is your 3-wood, and in either case you should still put your driver in the garage because it's only going to do evil things to your game.

That's clear enough, isn't it?

# Myth #8
# There is no way a club's design can reduce your slice. Only lessons can do that.

*Au contraire,* fellow lover of this great game—that statement is most certainly not true.

Can a golf club *cure* your slice? No, not even the magic of my custom fitted club designs can do that (harrumph!). Can it be reduced so your weekly donation to golf ball company sales is a little more within your budget? You bet; but, again, it's not something you're likely to find on the shelf over at the mega golf store. It's yet another reason why God created professional clubmakers.

Let's start with why you're slicing in the first place. It's happening because your clubface is meeting the ball in a slightly open position. That causes the ball to slide, then roll, across the face from the heel toward the toe, which in turn causes the ball to leave the face with its direction of backspin rotation tilted like a guy trying to stagger to his friend's car after his sixth martini. That, in turn, causes it to curve like it had eyes, toward the trees, rough, water, or other nastiness lurking to the right of the fairway—sometimes *far* to the right of the fairway. (Okay, the port side for you southpaws!)

To get rid of this dreaded blight on your game, you *can* take a few lessons. I would never want to discourage anyone from doing that. But the slice seems to be as resistant to cure as the common cold. In 2006, *Golf Digest* noted that 70 percent of all golfers slice the ball. With 27 million people chasing the ball around green pastures, that means that if you slice the ball you have 18,899,999 fellow golfers with whom you can commiserate. Now you know why it seems that every other issue of your favorite golf magazine has an article purporting to eliminate the same slice they guaranteed would be eliminated two issues previously.

So, what's a body to do?

As I said above, I can't stop slices from happening with my club designs—well, actually, I could, but the USGA would have a case of the vapors over the resulting club—but I can reduce its severity for most slicers. I can do it by using what's called an offset hosel and a closed face angle design.

No, it's not magic and it really is USGA legal, but you have to know what to look for and where to look for it. Let me take each of those in turn.

A conventional hosel (the cylinder sticking up from the head that the shaft goes into) is put on the head so that the clubface is a little in front of it. An offset hosel is positioned the other way around, so that the hosel is a little in front of the clubface. This does two things—both of them good.

If you hook the ball, you can immediately advance to the next myth. Do not pass GO; do not collect $200; and, whatever you do, do NOT play with an offset clubhead. If you do, you could develop a hook that is so bad your drives could wind up traveling full circle and hitting you in the left hindquarter.

For us slicers, however, things are different.

First, the more offset that is built into the clubhead, the farther the head's center of gravity (CG) will be located back from the shaft. And the farther the CG is back from the shaft, the higher the trajectory will be for any given loft on the face. In other words, if you have trouble getting the ball up in the air, this will help you a little.

Second, the more offset in the clubhead, the more time you have on the downswing to rotate the face of the clubhead back around and get it square (less open) to the target line. True, we're talking split seconds here, but sometimes that's enough to convert a banana slice into what you can claim to your friends is a "Jack Nicklaus power fade."

But suppose your Jack Nicklaus power fade is still putting you in the weeds? What then? What you can do is combine your offset hosel with a "hook face angle."

A hook-faced clubhead is one that has a more closed face angle. In other words, if you're a right-handed golfer and you set a hook-faced driver flat on its sole, the face would be pointed slightly in toward the left side of the target line. (Vice versa for the 8 percent of you who play from the other side of the ball.) So let's combine these two features and run some numbers.

Let's say that when you are using your conventional driver, your clubface is arriving 4 degrees open and creating a slice that's as big as all outdoors. So, with an offset hosel, that offset gives you an extra split second to rotate your hands, and the face is only open, say, two degrees when it meets the ball.

Well, that's certainly an improvement, but you want more.

Okay, so next you get a driver with an offset hosel *and* a 2-degree hook face built in. You make your swing; the offset hosel allows you to close the clubface 2 degrees; and the hook-faced clubface is *already* cocked 2 degrees inward.

Presto. Your 4-degree open face has been corrected, and you'll hit a nice straight shot. Neat, huh?

But what happens if your legendary ability to open the clubface at impact is greater than 4 degrees? Let's say it's 6 degrees.

Okay, the offset hosel will correct it, again say 2 degrees, and the hook face 2 more. Doesn't that still leave you with a 2-degree open face? Yup, it sure does! Remember, I told you at the beginning that proper clubfitting probably won't *cure* your slice; but, you gotta admit, going from 6 degrees open to 2 degrees open is one heck of an improvement. It will definitely increase your "swings per lost golf ball" statistic, not to mention giving you the real possibility of lowering your score.

There are a couple of caveats associated with all this. First, these built-in corrections work much better with woods than with irons. But that's probably okay because you slice your woods more than you do your irons. And, second, you have to resist defeating the correction capability of the club with your setup. In other words, until you get used to it, when you put a hook-faced club behind the ball it's going to look weird. It will look like it's aimed wrong, and you'll want to correct it by either pressing your hands forward or rotating the club in your hands. Don't do it. Your hook-faced club is simply being what it is supposed to be—a hook-faced club. Let it sit behind the ball, as it was designed to, so it can do its job of overcoming the open face you create in your swing.

All things considered, it's more than worth a try. I can tell you with the utmost confidence that a face angle and hosel offset change will result in the single biggest improvement a slicer will ever see in how they hit the ball.

But chances are you won't find these kinds of clubs on the shelf at the big box golf store because the big companies don't like to make closed-face or offset woods. That would require the retailers to explain to their customers why the club "looks funny." In turn, that would require the sales people to actually *know* why the club "looks funny," which would require the stores to spend more than 8.5 seconds in golf club training for their sales staff, which would … well, you get the point.

You'll probably need to go to a professional clubmaker, and even then he or she might have to special order the parts.

But ask, and eventually ye shall receive. And, who knows? Your slice might turn into that "Jack Nicklaus power fade" after all.

# Myth #9
# To hit the ball higher, use a club with a low center of gravity.

Yes, I know, you're scratching your head on this one. I mean, you've always been taught that a low center of gravity (CG) on a clubhead makes it easier to get the ball up in the air. That was one of the reasons for the cavity-back iron, wasn't it? By moving all that metal from the back-center of the club down low, you brought the center of gravity of the clubhead below the center of gravity of the ball, thus making it easier to hit.

Well, that's what I thought too—until I started designing more and more different kinds of clubheads and did more and more testing to watch and learn what makes the ball fly this way or that.

In my time I've designed well over a hundred different sets of irons and have tried everything I could to shove the CG significantly lower. Nothing has worked, at least not enough to make a big difference in the ball's launch angle, but it took me a while to figure out why.

It seems I was playing with the wrong variable. It turns out that it doesn't matter nearly as much how high or low the center of gravity is. You can't do much about that anyway, unless you feel comfortable playing with a clubhead that isn't much taller than a hot dog on the end of a stick. What matters more is how far the center of gravity is moved back from the face and the shaft.

I'll show you what I mean.

Let's say you take all the 5-irons that are currently on the market and measure their vertical CG height. You won't see a difference of more than 3 to 4 mm (one-sixth of an inch) from the highest of the high to the lowest of the low. This is true because all companies today are pretty much trapped by the head size (height mostly) that their irons need to have to look pleasing to their customers. No one is making big oversize irons anymore, and no one is making the little Browning 440-style/hot-dog-on-a-stick type of iron either. The public just won't buy either extreme.

As a result, virtually all 5-irons made today have a clubhead height at the toe end of the head of 53 to 57 mm and a height over on the heel side of the head that is proportional to that. In iron design you can try to make the sole wider or thicker to pull down the CG, but—no matter what—blade height rules. It controls the final vertical CG position more than any other design aspect. As long as the head is completely made from some grade of steel and the head heights are what they are today, you can't change the vertical CG position enough to make any real difference in launch angle.

But what about woods? Surely things must be different in those designs.

No, it's not—at least not among today's grapefruit-on-a-stick, 460cc jumbo drivers. With vertical CG, it's the same problem. But with drivers you have a lot more space to work with, and that makes all the difference. You see, what I learned is that where the center of gravity is located (up or down) doesn't ultimately matter nearly as much as where it is located front to back. With an iron, there's hardly any rearward place for the CG to move. With a driver there is.

Moving the CG rearward has more of a visible effect on trajectory than does vertical CG. This is because the rearward CG acts to make the *shaft* bend forward before impact, which increases the loft relative to the ground. The vertical CG's effect depends on how you swing the clubhead to meet the ball. Those are two very different things.

If you hit *down* on the ball with a low-CG head, that's good. In theory it means the line of force of your shot will be underneath the center of gravity of the ball, which will cause it to go up in the air. I say "in theory" because when you hit down on the ball you're also de-lofting the clubface, so most of the "hit it higher" things that happen as a result of your swinging downward at the ball are, at least partially, washed out.

That never happens if, instead of worrying so much about how high or low the center of gravity is, you simply find a clubhead with a CG that lies more rearward. You see, sooner or later on every swing you have to unhinge your wrists to let the clubhead go through the ball. When you do that, the head gains a final burst of speed so that it is, for a split second, actually running ahead of the shaft instead of lagging behind. It literally bends the shaft forward, and that's where the magic happens.

The farther back the clubhead CG is located, the more the shaft will bend forward. The more it bends forward, the more loft there is on the clubhead relative to the ground when impact occurs. By the way, for you gorillas who reach triple digits for your swing speed, this is why you see the ball fly higher when you hit your wife's clubs with their much more flexible shafts. Your higher swing speed bends the more flexible ladies' shaft farther forward, which increases the loft at impact. The more the loft is increased when the head hits the ball, the higher the ball will fly. Simple, no?

That's why you see so many more different designs cropping up with woods than you do with irons—because with woods you have more room in the larger-size heads to do something. With irons, as long as golfers don't like the hot-dog-on-the-stick style of head, you're pretty much stuck, and the available amount of weight you can move low on the head is just not going to make much of a difference in how high you hit the ball.

Besides, since loft affects shot height FAR more than the CG position, and since the industry has been feeding you a steady diet of irons with terminal cases of vanishing loft disease, it's no wonder the original promise of "low CG" falls well short of really making the ball easy to get up in the air.

# Myth #10
# The higher a clubhead's moment of inertia (MOI), the straighter the shot.

This myth is interesting because it is the unintended result of a USGA rule change. But let me start at the beginning.

You're probably familiar with the United States Golf Association as the organization that writes and maintains the Rules of Golf here in the United States and Mexico. You probably also know it is the organization that stages the U.S. Open golf tournament each year. What you might not know (prior to reading this book) is that it has a third role. It is the association's self-imposed responsibility to be the guardian of the equipment with which you play the game. More specifically, its duty is to make sure that "technology does not replace skill in the game."

Now, don't get me wrong. The USGA is a fantastic organization that does a huge amount for the game, and I applaud its efforts in many areas. But in the past ten years its equipment rule-making edicts have been utterly frustrating to me as a serious golfer and serious golf equipment designer. This is primarily because its rulings too often seem to lack consistency, and often seem to lack any grounding in scientific evidence. The current limits, for example, on COR, head size, club length, and MOI were adopted without any testing to scientifically determine their *real* effect on shot making. It's a theme I will come back to often in this book, but for now let me focus on the issue of moment of inertia or MOI.

In 1998, the USGA put a clamp on the spring face effect of clubheads by legislating a limit for the Coefficient of Restitution (COR) of clubfaces. Next, they capped the size of driver heads at 460cc because … well, I am not sure why, unless some of the USGA decision makers were embarrassed at seeing yet larger heads showing up at their venerable golf courses. After that, they set a limit specifying that no golf club could ever be longer in length than 48 inches. (Actually that rule does you a favor, since it tells you, me, and every other golfer that we don't have a prayer of being able to hit consistently a driver of any longer length—nor any driver even close to it!)

The latest in the USGA's campaign to make life miserable for us designers is a limit on the Moment of Inertia (MOI) of the driver head. However, the rule makers created an unintended consequence by setting an MOI limit that is *much* greater than what any company has ever been able to achieve, at least as of the 2008 writing of this book. That created a problem because it sent a message to golfers that said, in effect: the higher the MOI, the more the sanctity of the game is potentially compromised by making it "too easy."

As a result, by the time you read this, I'd be willing to bet you'll be reading ads by companies saying their driver is right at the "legal MOI limit." Bigger number, better driver, more sales, right? Well, that's how it works if you are a company that needs to hit ten-figures in annual sales to prevent your stock prices from falling. In fact, however, it simply is not true.

You might remember from our discussion in Myth #4 that MOI is measured in units called "grams centimeter squared" and that some of the new square- or triangular-shaped drivers that are now all the rage are claiming an MOI between 5,000 and 5,250 g-cm$^2$. Is that a good thing? It must be, otherwise why would the USGA attempt to limit it, right?

Well, you be the judge. Here are the facts on those big square drivers with an MOI number north of 5,000.

- First, a driver with an MOI measurement of 5,000 is only some 300 to 800 MOI units higher than the 460cc drivers made one to four years previously.
- Second, it takes an increase of 1,400 MOI units to make a driver twist *one-half degree less* in response to an off-center hit.

- Third, a higher MOI has nothing—absolutely nothing—to do with the performance of an on-center hit.
- Fourth, if your new 5,000-plus MOI driver were to somehow get even larger and manage to resist off-center hit twisting by that whopping half-degree, frankly, you wouldn't even notice it.
- Fifth and finally, since almost every one of the 5,000 MOI drivers are 45–46 inches in length with less than 12 degrees of loft and a standard everything else, you would do yourself a *bigger* favor by simply being properly fitted in the first place. If you do that, you won't need that shoebox-on-a-stick because you won't be hitting the ball off center as much.

Somehow, though, I don't think this information will be making it into those golf club ads any time soon.

# Myth #11
# The loft and lie angles on your irons are okay. They were set at the factory.

So you've just arrived home from the big box golf store with your new set of clubs. They are shiny, never-been-hit beauties, and they're great clubs. You know they're great because: (a) you paid the gross national product of a third-world nation for them; (b) they are a "prestigious brand name"; and (c) they are "just like the ones the pros use." (More about *that* later!)

Let me start by saying that in general the big golf companies do a wonderful job, from a purely engineering standpoint, of designing the individual components of their golf clubs. But the question I am trying to get you to ask is: how well are those off-the-rack clubs matched to *your* size, strength, athletic ability, and swing characteristics? If you answered: "They must be, they're a well-known brand name," then it's time for a further dose of reality.

As we will cover in more detail later on, you have to keep in mind that few of the major club companies actually *make* anything—most are essentially design and marketing firms—and some are not even that. Some are pure marketing firms that allow the foundry (or someone else) to design and build the clubs they sell.[3]

So your clubheads were, in all likelihood, physically manufactured in a place whose name you can't pronounce, by people who

---

[3] There is only one U.S. company (that I know of) that still makes at least some of its own heads, and that is PING.

might or might not even know what a golf club is, and whose monthly salary is not even one-fourth of what you paid for the clubs. Given that, do you think it might be worth a few minutes and maybe a few bucks to see if your clubs are set up the way they're supposed to be? It's important, and here's why.

There are no established standards in the golf industry for length, loft, lie, shaft flex, or just about anything else. It is a "standard made, mass produced, one-size-fits-all" market, and what you don't know *can* hurt you. Take the issue of loft.

The loft of a club is basically how far the face of the clubhead is tilted back. Every club, including the putter, has a different loft angle. That's the main reason we hit the ball a different distance with each club in our bag.

Cavity-back irons (which are probably what you have) will typically have less loft per same head number than will forged, carbon steel irons. For example, the 5-iron from a cavity-back model will typically be in the area of 25 to 26 degrees, while the 5-iron from a traditional forged carbon steel set will typically have a loft angle of 27 to 28 degrees.

The critical factor in this myth is not so much what the lofts are, but rather whether the lofts are evenly separated from each other. You see, if the lofts of your clubs are not spaced consistently apart, you won't have a consistent distance difference between the clubs.

All clubheads of quality, regardless of make or model, are manufactured to a loft tolerance of plus-or-minus 1 degree. That might sound sloppy to you, but let me assure you that no clubhead production factory on Planet Earth can make millions of heads all with exactly the same loft (or lie angle, or face angle, or headweight, etc.). And no, I am not exaggerating when I say millions. There are more than ten clubhead production factories that each make well over a million clubheads per year, and some forty more that make between 500,000 and a million per year. That's a *lot* of clubheads to produce with complete accuracy.

So, let's say you had three clubs with lofts as follows:

| Club | Loft | Separation |
|------|------|------------|
| 7-iron | 34 degrees | 4 degrees |
| 8-iron | 38 degrees | 4 degrees |
| 9-iron | 42 degrees | |

Okay, that's perfect. Each iron is 4 degrees away from its neighbor, which is the way they should be for most male golfers to ensure a 10- to 15-yard distance between adjacent clubs.

But let's say, *within accepted manufacturing tolerances,* that the 7-iron is 1 degree higher (35 degrees), the 8-iron is 1 degree lower (37 degrees), and the 9-iron is 1 degree higher (43 degrees) than they should be. (This is, by the way, not an unrealistic occurrence at all for even the very best clubhead foundries.)

| Club | Error | Loft | Separation |
|------|-------|------|------------|
| 7-iron | +1 degree | 35 degrees | 2 degrees |
| 8-iron | −1 degree | 37 degrees | 6 degrees |
| 9-iron | +1 degree | 43 degrees | |

So the separation between the 7- and the 8-iron is now 2 degrees, and the separation between the 8- and the 9-iron is now 6 degrees. To put that into context: for the average-to-above-average male golfer, a 4-degree separation in short iron lofts should generate a 10- to 15-yard difference in distance. With a 2-degree spacing, you're looking at only a 5–7 yard difference, while with 6 degrees, the two clubs will differ by about 15 to 22 yards.

Now, suppose the company you bought your clubs from is less finicky than my company and a few others. Let's say, to keep costs down, they chose to work with a head production factory that can't do any better than a manufacturing tolerance of plus or minus *2* degrees. That's only one lousy degree of difference, right? But look at what happens.

| Club | Error | Loft | Separation |
|------|-------|------|------------|
| 7-iron | +2 degrees | 36 degrees | 0 degrees |
| 8-iron | −2 degrees | 36 degrees | 8 degrees |
| 9-iron | +2 degrees | 44 degrees | |

The separation between the 8- and the 9-iron is now 8 degrees (!), and the separation between the 7- and the 8-iron is ZERO! *They are the same club!* The only difference is that the 8-iron will be a half-inch shorter, which in terms of shot distance is nothing. Only when a length difference between irons is 1 inch or longer will club length begin to matter for shot distance.

Have you ever had two clubs of different numbers that seem to hit the ball pretty much the same distance no matter what you do? Or maybe two clubs with adjacent numbers that hit the ball so much differently in distance from each other that you think you're missing a club? Well, now you know the probable reason why. If you want clubs that give you consistently distinct distances, they have to have consistently spaced lofts.

Fortunately, the golf gods have smiled on us, at least in this one area. They made most iron heads readily adjustable for the loft and the lie angles. To correct your clubs, all you need to do is take them to a professional clubmaker. For very little cost he or she will measure the *actual* loft of your clubs and bend the offending ones back to where they should be.

And while you're at it, don't forget to have the lie angle—the angle at which the shaft enters the clubhead—fitted to *your indi- vidual* size and swing as well (see Myth #27 for an eye-opener about *that*). The same set you bought off the rack in the pro shop or golf store has also been sold to about 100,000 other people. What do you think the probability is that the factory lie angle is the correct one for *all* of them, including you? In other words, do you suppose that all 100,001 golfers who bought this set are the same height, or have the same arm length, posture, set-up, and swing mechanics as you? One size fits all?

Nope, so when you take your irons in, have the clubmaker determine the proper lie angle for you as well. The test to deter- mine the correct lie angle for each club for *your* game is quick, painless, and accurate. Your clubs can easily be adjusted for lie at the same time your clubmaker is adjusting the lofts.

Not only should you do this with any new set of clubs, but if you're a strong divot taker or you pound balls off range mats a lot, you should also have your old set checked at least once a year. With forceful use, even a perfectly calibrated set can be stressed enough from repeated impacts with the ground/mats to go out of whack.

It's a small price to pay to help make an already difficult game a little easier.

# Shafts

# Myth #12

# You are using stiff shafts (or any other flex) in your clubs. It says so right on them.

Sorry, my friend, but my guess is that you have no idea what flex you have in the shafts of your golf clubs. You see, the "S" flex code (or X, R, A, or L) you see on your shaft is virtually meaningless.

Most golfers know, or think they know, that shafts come in a variety of flexes: X for extra stiff, S for stiff, R for regular, A for amateur or senior, and L for ladies'. What most golfers don't realize is that those letters (and only those letters) represent just about everything upon which there is universal agreement when it comes to the flex of your shafts.

You say you want a "stiff" shaft in your driver? Fine. Whose definition of "stiff" do you want to use? Because one shaft company's "stiff" is another company's "regular," which is another company's "A-flex." Worse, the flex rating of one model of shaft might be at hopeless variance with that of another model, even within the same shaft or golf club company!

And I'm just getting started.

Is that "stiff" shaft going into an iron or a wood? Because iron "stiffs" are stiffer than wood "stiffs." And you've said nothing about whether you want that driver in a steel shaft whose "stiff" is almost always different from a "stiff" graphite shaft.

If you're thinking the concept of shaft flex is hosed to the point of insanity, you are exactly right. If you buy a golf club because it has a stiff, regular, senior, or ladies' flex shaft in it, you have *no idea* what you're getting—nor does anyone else.

Shaft flex is defined as the overall average resistance of the shaft to bending. Now, you might know that resistance by its general letter designation, but some designers and clubmakers know it in a different way. We have systematically measured the *actual* stiffness of each shaft and translated those numbers into swing speed ratings. Some of us can even measure the actual stiffness in the grip end, center, and clubhead end of the shaft as well. That's why when you get a set of professionally custom fitted clubs built by a *really good* custom clubmaker, one of the first things the clubmaker will measure is your swing speed. He or she will then start the fitting process by considering only shafts whose flex corresponds within a narrow range to your specific swing speed, and then apply other factors, such as your swing movements, to the stiffness of the grip, center, and head portions of the shaft, to come up with a final recommendation.

What makes it tricky is that shafts of the same letter flex do not necessarily have the same swing speed ratings. You'd think it would be that way, but nope, there are no standards in the golf industry specifying the stiffness of each letter flex, so each shaft maker and golf club company is free to define its flexes any way it wants to. The S-flex from one company might be for a golfer with an 80–90 mph swing speed, while the S-flex from another is designed for a 90–100 mph golfer. The same goes for all the other flex letters! Even different shaft models of the same flex within the same company do not necessarily agree with each other.

It's an interesting way to make one of the central equipment components for an entire industry, isn't it? Try doing that in any other sport! In tennis, where string tension is a racket's equivalent of shaft flex in a golf club, string tension is measured and set in pounds per square inch of force, so when you get a new racket and have your strings set at the same 55 pounds as the strings in your old racket, you'll be playing with the same "flex" that you're used to. Not so in golf, however.

It gets even worse when it comes to seniors, women, and worst of all *senior women*. (By the way, have you ever seen a club or shaft marketed toward the senior lady golfer? Right. Like senior ladies don't play golf?)

In one shaft flex study *every* ladies' shaft tested was out of sequence compared to the other A, R, S, and X shaft flexes. Most were too stiff, especially when cut and installed to the shorter assembly length of standard women's clubs. Given the importance of shaft stiffness in helping to get the ball up in the air, this is a serious problem. It means that most female golfers—especially senior females—might be having their game actively hindered by the shafts they're using.

Recently, a few shaft companies have come out with what they call an "LL-Flex." Translated, the LL-flex means: "We finally figured out there are differences in lady golfers' swing speeds just like there are with men, so we decided to finally do what we do for men and give you different stiffness options." The thing is, these additional women's flex shafts are pretty much used only by custom clubmakers who buy shafts in component form and then identify which women need the more flexible or more stiff models. That's why senior women especially need to consider seeing a good professional clubmaker to get the best match of clubs to their size, strength, athletic ability, and swing characteristics. What's available in standard form, off the rack in the golf retail stores just doesn't cover the range of what most senior men or women need to play their best.

As for you younger male golfers, here's the bottom line. *From a pure shaft performance standpoint, 90 percent of you are going to be better off with a shaft that is more flexible than what you think you need.*

More specifically, if you happened to end up in a shaft that's too stiff for your swing speed and your swing mechanics, first, the ball will go a little shorter in distance because it will probably fly a little lower. Second, you might have a tendency to see the ball fly over to the fade side of the target, and your feeling from hitting the ball on the center of the face will be a little more "harsh," as if the club were vibrating a little more. Third, because the shaft is too stiff for your swing, you'll start swinging harder to try to "flex the shaft" more and that will result in a higher percentage of off-center, distance-robbing, and accuracy-deficient shots.

On the other hand if you happened to end up with a shaft that's too flexible for your swing, first, the ball might fly a little higher, and from that possibly a little farther. Second, it might cause a fade shot to fade a little less or a draw shot to draw a little more, and the feeling of an on-center impact on the clubface will impart a soft but nevertheless solid feeling. Only if you have a fundamentally solid swing with an inside/out swing path and late unhinging of the wrist cock on the downswing would you ever come close to drawing the ball more than you want with a shaft that is too flexible. For the rest of the golf swings, the other 80 percent of all golfers—nope, erring on the side of more flexible shafts is good, not bad.

For the majority of us golfers, having more flexible shafts is a no-brainer.

Next, unless you work with a professional clubmaker to make your shaft selection, you will have to do a lot of trial-and-error test hitting of all sorts of shafts before you come up with a decision—and that could be hazardous to your pocketbook.

You might be able to guess that you want to have an R- or an S-flex for example. But a problem arises, as I mentioned above, because the R from one company can be very different in stiffness from the R of another. You then have no other alternative but to (a) do trial-and-error testing to see for yourself how stiff or flexible that new R- or S-flex shaft really is compared to your old one; or (b) listen to a retail salesperson who nine times out of ten won't know enough about shafts to really ensure you get the right one for your swing.

You might be measured for your swing speed in a retail golf store, but I am here to tell you that virtually *none* of the major golf club companies ever provide their retailers with a reference chart to indicate what swing speed matches up with which flex in each shaft model they offer. So, the recommendation of the retail salesperson will quite possibly be a guess, or will be based on which flex they have more of in their store inventory at the moment.

The proper way to do it is to have a competent clubmaker measure your swing speed, then observe your swing mechanics to look for things like your tempo, how much force you use to start the downswing, and where in the downswing you unhinge your wrists. The clubmaker will then ask you some questions about how high or low you hit the ball with different clubs and other performance questions to determine what real shotmaking improvements could be associated with the shaft's performance for *your* game.

He or she will then reference the files of shaft information that come from suppliers or from research on shaft testing that clubmakers have done and made available to each other. He or she will also have more precise lists of what swing speed matches well to what shaft flex, for what shaft design.

After that, the clubmaker will make a recommendation and possibly build a test club for you to hit to obtain feedback. The shop might also have a launch monitor that can be used to actually measure the launch angle contribution of the shaft as you swing the club. And in the end, the clubmaker will come up with a far more accurate recommendation of which shaft is likely to perform and feel best to *you*.

# Myth #13
# The shaft is the engine
# of the golf club.

I wish I had a dollar for every time I've read or heard this statement in my career. We'd almost be talking retirement money
here.

To say that the shaft is the engine of the golf club is to imply
that the shaft is the most important component. After all, how
well would your car perform without an engine? But, no matter
how much you might want to believe that statement, the shaft is
*not* the most important component of the golf club, and I mean
*any* golf club from the driver to the putter.

First, I truly believe all the components of the club and how
they work together are important, but if you forced me to vote
for one component as more important than the others, I would
vote for the clubhead and not the shaft. I know there are some of
you who have just wrinkled your brows, so here's why I believe
that.

Let's try a little experiment. You pick any shaft that you are
sure would be a very poor shaft for you to use. Too heavy, too
stiff, it doesn't matter what type of ill-suited shaft you choose.
I'll bet the farm I can pick a clubhead to go with that shaft and
build a club with which you will get very good results for both
distance and accuracy. Then, I'll ask you to bring me a shaft that
you know from experience is a very good fit for your swing. I'll
select a clubhead to go with that shaft, build the club, and bet
that that club will result in such poor performance that you won't
ever want to hit with that club more than once.

Not fair, you say, because you know I could pick a clubhead
with 6 degrees of loft and a 4-degree closed face angle to go with
your perfect shaft? Fine, then you can pick any XX-flex, 130-gram

shaft with 1 degree of torque for the poor fitting example in this experiment. I bet I can *still* find a clubhead and build a club that will allow you to experience far better shotmaking results than the club built with your all-time favorite shaft. Granted, the club with the wrong shaft and right head might not feel that good when you hit the ball, but the distance and accuracy will be far better than with the other club.

So what's my point here? Am I trying to tear down the contribution of the shaft to the fitting success of the golf club? Not at all. I am simply trying to place the importance of the shaft for *real* performance in its proper priority for the vast majority of golfers.

The shaft *is* important, but not nearly as important as the clubhead specs and the way the club is assembled—length, swingweight, and so forth. It is not the "engine" that some people would have you believe. It's more like the transmission. You, the golfer, are the engine.

# Myth #14
## The shaft acts like a buggy whip. It gives additional speed to the ball with its last-second snap.

Over the past three years my engineering staff and I have spent a lot of time digging deeply into the subject of what the shaft does and how it does it during the swing. We've done this through computer analysis and experimentation, as well as with hit testing, high-speed cameras, and launch monitor analysis with different golfers.

Our goal is to create a model that will fully simulate golf shaft performance, but our work is far from completed. We do believe, however, that we are at a point where we understand shaft performance more clearly than it has ever been known before. So, let me start by telling you what the shaft does NOT do in the swing.

Many, in fact most, serious golfers (and even clubmakers) think that the shaft "loads" up energy from its initial bending at the start of the downswing and then "unloads" in a buggy-whip or spring action to slingshot the ball down the fairway.

I'm here to tell you that this is not how the shaft works. But don't feel bad; I used to think the same thing until we really started to look into the subject. I mean heck, when you make a mind's-eye picture of the bending of the shaft in the swing, it seems logical that the shaft should work like a slingshot or a catapult. Bend it back and let it spring forward to launch the ball. As I said, it used to make sense to me too.

If you have ever seen a swing robot in operation, whether in the flesh or in video, you might notice that these "hitting robots" almost always hit the ball using only a downswing. Why is that?

For one, it's because it is an incredibly complex engineering task to design and build a robot to swing like we humans do. But the main reason they do not have a backswing is that they don't need one. It's the downswing (only) that determines the outcome of every shot, and that's what the engineers are interested in.

This might seem confusing to you because you know your slice happens when you open the clubface during the backswing. That might be true, but if you learned how to close the clubface on the downswing to offset the accuracy damage you do on the backswing, everything would come out fine. Believe me, the downswing is where it all happens. In the real world, however, we humans need a backswing to synchronize the swing rhythm and timing for our bodies and to create enough momentum to enable us to reach maximum controllable swing speed.

But this robot testing has created the common belief that the shaft "loads" and then "unloads," acting like a buggy whip. That's a myth. If it were true, every golfer would be using a very flexible shaft and playing crack-the-whip on every shot.

Does the shaft bend? Of course it does. Depending on the actual stiffness design of the shaft and the amount of force applied by the golfer to start the downswing, the shaft will bend because there is a mass out on the end of it (the clubhead) that wants to resist the change in direction. The greater the amount of force applied by the golfer in the downswing, the greater the mass of the clubhead, the more flexible the shaft, and the stronger the golfer's wrists and hands, then the more the shaft will bend once we start the downswing. This combination of factors is what has been called "loading" the shaft.

But here's where things get interesting.

Look at the figure on the next page and think about what you're seeing. When the golfer starts the downswing, it is led with the *heel* of the clubhead—not the face—so any bending that takes place will occur along the back of the shaft, and that's no help to our buggy-whip theory. That also means that at some point prior to impact we have to rotate the clubhead 90 degrees to get the clubface looking down the target line again. To do that, we (obviously) need to use our hands, and that's where the "buggy whip" disappears.

Our hands are supple, fleshy, and not even close to being able to hold on to the grip as rigidly as an iron vise. If our hands were completely rigid like a bench clamp, there could be a "spring back" action on a golf shaft during the swing. But no matter how strong you think your hands are, they cannot, and will not, do anything but act like a shock absorber during the swing to dampen the bending action of the shaft.

Try it yourself if you don't believe me. Grip your driver as tightly and rigidly as you possibly can while a friend pulls back the head to bend the shaft. Once your friend lets go of the head, the shaft simply returns to a straight position as your hands move in a natural reaction to completely absorb the force. That's what automatically happens during the swing.

It's true you might have seen some photos of the clubhead shooting ahead of the shaft just before impact. But that's not because the shaft is whipping the clubhead along. It's because, at the last second, the golfer has unhinged his wrist-cock angle, which slows down the arms and speeds up the clubhead, thus allowing the clubhead to bend the shaft forward just before impact with the ball.

The better the golfer's swing fundamentals and the more refined the golfer's sense of feel for detecting the movement of the club and shaft during the swing, the more important the shaft becomes to the total performance of the golf club. I'll give you an example of what I mean.

Even with semi-decent swing mechanics and many years of playing the game, I bet if you hit balls with a driver that has a very flexible shaft, you'll figure out eventually that to hit the ball with consistency, you have to *slow things down a little* to achieve more ball-striking success.

But what happens when you ramp up your swing with that very flexible driver to your full power level? You can't hit the ball as consistently long and straight and solidly because you depend on the shaft for a big part of your overall swing timing and rhythm. *That,* my friends, is precisely why getting a properly fitted shaft is so important.

With the right shaft, golfers who can feel differences between shafts can time the power of a swing so comfortably that they actually gain swing speed and distance from being able to completely "freewheel" the club through the ball, There is absolutely no artificial manipulation needed—and such manipulation usually only gets in the way.

For golfers with a sense of feel that allows them to note bending differences in the shaft during the swing, having the right shaft is like being able to shift a car engine into a higher gear.

# Myth #15
# The faster you swing, the stiffer your shaft should be.

At several points in this book I mention that a good golf club maker will, at some point, measure your swing speed. He or she will do that in order to narrow down your shaft possibilities to only those that have the appropriate amount of flex for that speed. You might then conclude that's the end of it. If you have a higher swing speed, you get a stiffer shaft, and a less stiff shaft if your swing speed is lower.

But it's not true. You see, that swing speed thing is only the *beginning* of the shaft fitting process, and, if it is done properly, you might wind up with a shaft that is quite different from what you might have originally thought.

If you've been reading these myths in order, you already know that: (a) the flex rating printed on your shaft means nothing; and (b) that the shaft does *not* act like a buggy whip to slingshot the ball down the fairway. So, if the flex of the shaft does not slingshot the ball down the fairway, what does it do?

Remember in the previous myth, right at the end, I mentioned that what looks like a buggy-whip effect is not caused by the shaft at all. It's caused when the golfer releases his wrist-cock during the downswing. Well, that's where the shaft's stiffness does its work. The purpose of shaft flex is to work in conjunction with your release move (along with the clubhead loft, the clubhead center of gravity, and whether you swing up, level, or down at the ball) to determine the final launch angle and trajectory of your shot. The flex also has a lot to do with the "feel" of the club both before and when it impacts with the ball; that's a huge part of shaft fitting for some golfers, but for now let's just stick with the wrist-cock release issue.

When you start your swing downward, as long as you keep your wrist-cock angle hinged, your arms and the club are both moving at the same speed. Once you start to unhinge the wrists, the arms slow down while the club accelerates to a higher speed. The clubhead, which has been lagging behind the shaft all this time, now shoots forward and actually pushes ahead of the shaft. That, in turn, causes the shaft to bend forward, which increases the loft at the moment of impact, which in turn increases the launch angle of the ball, which influences its trajectory, which ultimately affects the distance the ball will travel.

The thing is, not all swing speeds are "created equal."

Let's take three hypothetical golfers. One releases his wrists quite early in the downswing, the other in the middle, and the third at the very end. The golfer who releases too early will have his shaft bend forward too soon. This causes it to arrive at impact in a straight position, and all those aforementioned trajectory effects will be lost. It is far better to be the second golfer and release your wrists at the midpoint of the downswing, or, best of all, to be the third golfer who releases at the very end, a split second before impact.

The point here is that *all three of those golfers could have exactly the same measured swing speed*! But do you think they should all be using the same shaft? Not hardly.

But there is even more to it than that. To *really* get the proper shaft for your clubs you also need to consider how smoothly you make the transition from the end of the backswing to the start of the downswing, how forcefully you start the downswing, how quick your downswing tempo is, how great your clubhead acceleration is, and how consistently you do each of the above.

Plug those factors into the equation, along with the location of your wrist-cock release, and *then* you can select your shaft. Just saying "X swing speed = Y shaft flex" won't cut it.

Now, one more question before I let you go on to the next myth.

When you bought your set of clubs off the rack at the big box golf store by the freeway, how many of *your* specific swing factors do you think were represented in those clubs?

Or, maybe I should put it another way: how lucky did you feel that day?

# Myth #16
# If the flex of your shaft is too soft, you'll hook the ball, and if it's too stiff, you'll slice it.

Well, neither is true. As you learned in the previous myth, shaft flex is (or ought to be) linked to the force of your downswing and the timing of your wrist-cock release—among other factors. It's not a major cause of whether you hook or slice the ball. But what might influence your hook or slice is another factor called "torque," which has nothing to do with flex. Because most golfers have never heard of it, I'll introduce it here.

Watching a high-speed film of what happens to a clubhead during the swing is a little like watching sausage being made. It's not a pretty sight, even if the results are wonderful. The clubhead is bobbing all over the place. It lags behind the shaft, it shoots ahead, the toe flattens out, the head twists open—I tell you, it's ugly. Sometimes I think it's a miracle that anyone ever gets off a straight shot. But it's the "twisting open" part I want to focus on here.

All clubheads, no matter what shaft they are attached to, will try to twist open during the downswing. The shaft enters the clubhead at the heel, which means almost all of its weight is hanging out there, away from the shaft. When the shaft starts down, your downswing force will act on that weight, and the head will try to twist open. What keeps it from hopelessly flopping over is the shaft, and the degree to which the shaft will resist that twisting motion. This resistance is properly called the torsional stiffness of the shaft, but what the golf industry has decided to call "the torque of the shaft." Now, for you techie-types out there, I know that technically "torque" is the term that describes the actual force of twisting and is not really a term that should be used to describe an ability to *resist* the force of twisting.

Okay, so each shaft has a certain resistance to twisting the golf industry calls shaft torque. This is measured in degrees of rotation, and too much of it can be a bad thing.

In the early days of graphite shafts, the typical shaft was manufactured with 10 or more degrees of torque because the graphite shaft makers did not yet know how to make their shafts so they could better resist twisting. This was the main reason so few golfers in the 1970s and early 1980s could ever hit the ball consistently well with a graphite shaft, and the product almost died. The only golfers who could hit the ball with accuracy were those who possessed a very smooth downswing transition and swing tempo, and an early-to-mid-downswing release of the wrist-cock. In other words, people who exerted very little sudden force on the club during the downswing.

By the middle to late 1980s the graphite shaft makers discovered that by wrapping the graphite sheet layers at an angle to the center line of the shaft, they could improve the shafts' resistance to twisting. This newfound manufacturing capability triggered a competition to make shafts with fewer and fewer degrees of torque. But it was soon discovered that there could be too much of a good thing.

What they found out was that increasing the torsional stiffness of a shaft to a torque measurement of 2 degrees or less had the result of making the impact feel very harsh and less solid for all but the most powerful golfers. In other words, very low torque shafts were only well matched to golfers with a tendency to apply very high levels of downswing force in their swings. For everyone else, the result was a loss of feel and often a loss of distance too.

So, they went back to the drawing board and produced the modern graphite shaft, which can be bought in a wide variety of torque measurements.

In case you're wondering, steel shafts will also torque, but not quite as much as graphite, so it is less of a problem. The reason is that steel, when formed into a tube, simply has a much greater natural resistance to twisting than does graphite.

So now then, what does all this mean to you?

In theory, torque can be a problem. You don't want so much of it that your head flops open on the downswing, but you don't want too little of it either. Like everything else about the golf club, *it has to fit your unique swing.*

The more powerful and aggressive your downswing, the more the shaft is subjected to forces from the clubhead that cause it to twist. As a result, if you start the downswing with great force and swing hard at the ball, you should probably never use a shaft with more than 3 to 3.5 degrees of torque. On the other hand, if you have a smooth, passive downswing tempo and an early-to-mid-downswing release, you should probably never use a shaft with a torque with less than 4 degrees of torque. Fortunately, if you choose a shaft with a flex that is otherwise right for your swing characteristics, in all likelihood the correct torque will come with it.

For those of you who are still wondering about the stiffness (or lack thereof) causing you to slice or hook the ball, let me say this. There are golfers who fade the ball with too flexible of a shaft, just as there are golfers who hook the ball with one. The same thing is true of golfers with shafts that are too stiff. This is simply because the main thing that causes a hook or a slice is your swing path and whether your hands and arms deliver the clubface open or closed at impact with the ball. When misdirection problems arise from the flex not being well fitted to your swing, that's probably because of what the bending feel of the shaft does to screw up your swing timing and cause a change in your swing path or how you deliver the face of the clubhead to impact.

Most golfers who can detect that the flex is too stiff tend to react by swinging harder. Those with a shaft that is too flexible react by "trying to slow down." Either way, the golfer ends up trying to swing differently from what is natural or typical, and when that happens, the houses on both sides of the fairway may be in peril.

# Myth #17
# Graphite shafts hit the ball farther than steel.

I don't remember the last time I walked into a retail golf store and saw a driver that did *not* have a graphite shaft in it. Now, since the driver is supposed to be the longest hitting club in your bag, and they all have graphite shafts, then graphite shafts must hit the ball farther then steel, right?

Wrong. At least not for the reason you're probably thinking.

To begin with, when we're talking about golf clubs we use the term "weight" in two different ways. The first is "weight" as in the total weight of the golf club. In other words, you put the club on a scale and see how heavy it is in grams or ounces. The second "weight" is in the term "swingweight." This refers to the perceived heaviness of the head in relation to the rest of the club when you grip and swing the club. In this myth, we're going to be talking about weight in the first sense. We'll get to swingweight later.

Shafts for woods and irons exist in a weight range from as light as 40 grams (1.4 oz) all the way up to more than 130 grams (4.6 oz), with graphite shafts, as a group, being much lighter than steel. Obviously, which shaft you use will determine how heavy the total weight of your club will be. The theory is that the lighter the total weight of the club, the faster you'll be able to swing it. And the faster you swing it, the farther the ball will go.

So, in that sense—assuming the graphite shaft in your club is lighter than any steel alternative—then, yes, your graphite shaft will in theory hit the ball farther. But it's not because there is any inherent magic in the graphite. If you replaced your graphite with a steel shaft of the same weight, the ball would go just as far because you'd be able to swing it just as fast.

There are three major components that make up a golf club: the head, the shaft, and the grip. If you want to achieve a lighter club, the most likely way to achieve that is by swapping out the shaft. Yes, you could go with a lighter head (if you can find one), but that will also reduce your ability to feel where the head is located when you swing it and likely result in you hitting the ball everywhere on the face except the center. Not good. And yes, you could go with a lighter grip, but the weight savings there will be minimal.

Nope, if you want a lighter total weight to your club so you can swing it faster, your best bet is to go to a very lightweight graphite shaft.

That ends the good news; now comes the bad. (I'll bet you knew this was coming, huh?)

First, if you already have a graphite shaft in your driver, you probably have about all the weight savings you're going to get. Sure, you could probably replace it with an even lighter one, but the difference in weight will most likely not be enough to make a noticeable difference in your swing speed. Decades of clubfitting research has shown me that the new shaft has to be at least 30 grams (1.1 oz) lighter than the old one before a golfer's swing speed will increase enough to see an improvement in distance. Most companies already use a 65–70 gram graphite shaft in their standard off-the-rack drivers, so to achieve a noticeable difference, you'd have to replace it with a shaft in the low 30-gram range—and that shaft doesn't exist.

The second reason falls into the reality check category.

I can count on fewer than the fingers of one hand the number of people I've known whose golf swing was *too slow*. Is that you? Is that really what's holding you back as a golfer? If it is, then fine, by all means move to a lighter shaft. But I've seen far, *far*, more people getting into trouble because they were swinging out of their shoes, than because their swing was too slow.

So then, if most golfers' problem is *not* that they swing too slowly, what *are* all those super-lightweight graphite shafts doing among the drivers down at the big box golf store? For the more cynical among us, the words "profit margin" might spring to mind.

Ultimately, the most important thing about shaft weight is to get the one that best matches your physical strength and the force you exert in making the downswing at the ball. If you do that, regardless of what material the shaft is made from, you will hit the ball more on-center and with a more consistent swing timing—and *that,* my fellow golfers, is where you will get your maximum distance.

# The Assembled Club

# Myth #18

# The longer the length of a club, the farther you'll hit the ball.

This is a topic that's really a sore point with me.

If you wander into just about any golf retail store these days, you'll notice that the length of the men's drivers they're selling is almost always between 45 and 46 inches. It's been like that for years. Yet, from 2005 through 2007, the average driver length among all players on the PGA Tour was 44.5 inches.

Now, does that not strike you as being slightly odd? I mean, here are the best players on the planet—players for whom distance off the tee is absolutely critical to their game—and they are routinely using drivers that are *shorter* then the ones that are being peddled to you!

It turns out that the explanation is quite straightforward: *If those pros could hit the ball longer and straighter with a longer driver, they would; but they can't, so they don't.* Why? Because the longer driver is so much harder to hit accurately and consistently solidly, and if the best players on the planet can't hit a 45–46-inch driver solidly and accurately, what are the chances *you* can?

If clubheads have been suffering from vanishing loft disease, then the length of the driver has positively gone on anabolic steroids. It's a phenomenon that began to appear in the golf equipment industry in the 1980s, and it took off like Barry Bonds' biceps.

It's time to be brutally honest with you. The demand for longer driver length is 100 percent artificially created by the big golf companies' marketing departments to convince you that longer tee shots are only an inch or three away. To make matters worse, they are doing so without telling you any of the consequences or giving you any other options.

Have you ever leafed through a stack of golf magazines and noticed that just about every issue contains at least one article on "How to Get More Power" or "How to Hit for Greater Distance"? Did you notice also that on about every other page is a $70,000 ad for a driver that *promises* you "more power" or "greater distance"? Now my final question. Do you honestly think the two are unrelated?

Once again, when you put their hand on the Bible and keep them our of earshot from the marketing mavens of their companies, the designers and engineers who work for the major club brands know that longer clubs are much, *much* harder for the average golfer to hit. But the club companies are not run by designers and engineers. They are run by the sales and marketing departments, and therein lies the problem. Each year they have to have something "new and improved" to sell to be able to increase sales and keep their stockholders happy. Not every three years like it used to be, not every two years, every *year*.

The "new" part is fine, but when the word "improved" has lost all meaning—when changes are made that are actually *harmful* to the average golfer's game—then I have to draw the line. This is one of those cases.

In my estimation, the drivers sold in shops are too long for 90 percent of the men and women golfers who buy them. Let me tell you precisely who can successfully use one of the 45–46-inch drivers that populate the racks in every golf store on the planet.

If you are a golfer with a very smooth tempo, who swings consistently with an inside/out swing path, has a late release of your wrist-cock angle, and hits 13 out of 14 fairways a round, then you are in luck. Go right ahead and use that pole. If that's not you, then go get a new driver fitted and built from scratch; only this time don't just get it cut to the right length, but also get the shaft, loft, face angle, grip size, and swingweight that's best for your swing and how you play.

Here's why.

Let's start with the issue of distance. Most golfers believe that longer drivers generate a higher swing speed that allows you to

hit the ball farther. They won't. Twice in my career I have conducted tests with real golfers and drivers of different lengths to
see the effect of length on swing speed, distance, and ability to hit
the ball on center. I can assure you that the only golfers who can
swing longer drivers at a higher swing speed and still hit the ball
on center are those who are: (1) low handicappers, (2) very good
athletes with good hand/eye coordination, or (3) points 1 and 2
together, along with an inside-out swing path, a normal-to-flat
swing plane, a late wrist-cock release, and a smooth, rhythmic
swing tempo. In other words, it's only a very small percentage of
the golfing population. Every other golfer in the studies suffered
from an increase in off-center hits with no swing speed increase
at all as the driver length was increased.

The pros on tour know they can't hit the length of your driver
you bought off the rack as consistently on center or as straight as
they can one that is shorter. Believe me, they've all tried because
they play golf for a living and they all know how valuable another
10 or 20 yards off the tee can be to their bank accounts. They also
know how tough it can be to grow their bank accounts when half
the time they're hitting their second shot with the ball sitting in
four inches of rough. The irony is that, all the while, here you are
hitting most of your drives on the toe or heel, watching the ball
slice into the trees, praying you can make that one good swing,
and thinking the whole time that it's *your* fault.

But there's another reason for having a shorter driver. It
appears that, in the hands of real people, the shorter driver might
very well hit the ball, not just with more accuracy, but farther
as well.

For every half-inch by which you miss the sweet spot on your
driver, you lose up to ten yards in distance. Miss it by an inch,
and you might lose up to twenty yards. Conversely, if you can
gain enough control of the head to hit the ball even a half-inch
closer to the sweet spot, you'll gain back almost all the yardage
you *think* you're losing by using a shorter shaft. Add to that the
fact that 90 percent of all golfers do not possess swing mechanics
that could possibly gain an increase in swing speed from a longer length, and you have the reason most people end up hitting

shorter drivers farther. They're swinging at the same speed, but they're hitting closer to the sweet spot more often because the shorter driver is easier for them to control.

So, how do you know what is the right length for you?

First, the length of your clubs is not determined by your height; it's determined by a combination of your height plus the length of your arms, and then massaged from there to the final length by your swing path, swing tempo, swing plane, and individual ball striking ability.

The way a good clubmaker determines proper length is by first measuring the distance from your wrist to the floor and looking up that dimension on a chart to obtain an initial driver length recommendation (see chart below). After that, the clubmaker looks at your swing skill and athletic ability before coming up with a final length decision. But that's just the beginning.

Look at it this way. The Holy Grail in fitting golf clubs—especially a driver—is to get you the longest club you can swing *with*

**Wrist-to-Floor Measurement for Initial Club Lengths (inches)**

| Wrist-to-Floor | Driver Length | 5-Iron Length |
| --- | --- | --- |
| 27 to 29 | 42 | 36.5 |
| 29 to 32 | 42.5 | 37 |
| 32 to 34 | 43 | 37.5 |
| 34 to 36 | 43.5 | 38 |
| 36 to 37 | 44 | 38.25 |
| 37 to 38 | 44.25 | 38.5 |
| 38 to 39 | 44.5 | 38.75 |
| 39 to 40 | 44.75 | 39 |
| 40 to 41 | 45 | 39.25 |
| 41 to 42 | 45.5 | 39.5 |
| over 42 | 46 and up | 39.75 and up |

*Note:* A wrist-to-floor measurement is used as the initial guideline for determining club lengths that will match well with the golfer's height and arm length for comfort. To make the measurement correctly, wear flat-sole shoes only, stand comfortably erect, shoulders perfectly level, arms hanging relaxed at the sides. The measurement is made from the major wrist crease on the dominant hand to the floor in inches plus any fraction.

*control.* So, let's say your wrist-to-floor measurement says you should be using a 44-inch driver. Okay, that's fine if, and only if, you can consistently control a 44-inch club!

So the second step will be to give you a driver of that length and have you hit some balls—maybe with some marking tape on the club face to see your point of impact. By watching your swing and seeing the results, your clubmaker might make your club a little longer or a little shorter. In other words, your clubmaker will tinker until satisfied that he or she has indeed found the length that will result in the combination of your highest swing speed with the greatest on-center hit consistency. Remember, distance is as much about solid contact as anything else. If you would be better off with a shorter club, then go for it. *You will probably hit the ball just as far (if not farther) and with a lot more accuracy!*

Notice that these are all decisions that are best made by an experienced custom club fitter—not by the marketing department at some club company a thousand miles away. You see, as I pointed out in the introduction to this book, they have a problem. They have to make clubs as standard as possible so their retailers won't have to stock too many options in their store. At the same time, they have to convince you that you genuinely need whatever "new and improved" object they have to sell.

Don't let them make *their* marketing problem *your* golf problem.

# Myth #19
# Men's clubs should always be longer than women's clubs.

If I ever give up designing golf clubs, I think I might open a shoe store and run it like the golf industry. I'll have dozens of different shoe styles on display for both men and women. But all the men's shoes will be size 10 (the men's national average in the United States) and all the women's shoes will be one size smaller. Any customer who happened to fit those sizes would be in luck. If not … I'd start by telling him or her how popular the shoes were—how millions have been sold, whether they fit or not—and that they're "just like the ones the pros wear."

That makes perfect sense, doesn't it?

Proper clubfitting is androgynous. There are no male golfers; there are no female golfers; nor are there young golfers or old ones. There are only golfers. Each has to be assessed according to size, strength, athletic ability, and swing characteristics. Period. End of myth.

Don't let someone pigeonhole you into some kind of ridiculous national average—whether you are male *or* female.

# Myth #20

# Graphite-shafted irons need to be longer than steel-shafted ones.

Am I missing something here?

If you have a set of steel-shafted irons that are fitted and built to the correct length for your size, strength, athletic ability, and swing characteristics, why would you want to have a set of graphite-shafted irons that are built to the *incorrect* length? Or conversely, if your steel shafts are incorrect, how are things improved by making your graphite a longer version of "incorrect?"

Okay, okay … I'll calm down. I am not jumping on anyone. I know this is a common misconception, and, generally speaking, it's true that irons built with graphite shafts *are* sold in a standard length that is a half-inch longer than the steel-shafted versions. So it's logical for you to think that there must be a reason for that. Well, there is. It makes the clubs cheaper and easier to make.

What? Am I saying that the major club companies would compromise your game just to save a few extra bucks?

Please, don't even ask. Let me just go right into the story.

Earlier in this book I talked about the dreaded vanishing loft disease, whereby each year the clubhead lofts were made a little lower so the marketing departments could say the new clubs "hit farther." Well, very much like the lofts, club length has undergone a similar change.

At one time back in the 1960s and 1970s, virtually all golf club companies kept to the same lengths for each of the clubs in a set. However, starting in the 1980s, a number of companies began to break ranks and increase the lengths of their clubs, particularly for the woods. Once some of the companies began doing it, all the others were compelled to follow.

By the 1990s all woods (drivers in particular) had "grown" to a point where they were over two inches longer than they had been. This sudden and substantial increase in driver and wood length was not the result of some compelling design breakthrough. As I pointed out under Myth #18, it came from the marketing department. According to them, distance sells, so sell distance we shall.

The big companies were convinced that the longer the length, the faster the golfer would swing the club, and the farther the golfer would hit the ball. That the golfers would also be sending the balls farther into the trees and bordering back yards mattered not a bit. Manufacturers raced each other to push driver lengths to the point where they are now—2.5 to 3 inches longer than the length of drivers in the 1960s and 1970s, and in total disregard of the club design credo that says, "the longer the length, the harder the club will be to hit consistently solidly and on center."

So how does this relate to graphite club length? It has to do with something called "swingweight"—the perceived heaviness of the clubhead.

In the case of the irons, the major club companies increased length only by a half-inch per numbered club. This smaller increase in iron length was dictated by their recognition that irons primarily needed to be accurate, so they didn't dare trash the irons with *too* much length. Besides, it was just as easy to accomplish the same "increased distance" objective by making the iron heads with a lot lower loft and not tell anyone about it. After all, 99 percent of all golfers know their irons only by their numbers and not by their exact loft angles.

Nevertheless, when graphite shafts became more popular, the major club companies began to make their graphite-shafted irons a half-inch longer than their already elongated steel-shafted models. This led many golfers to assume that, for some performance reason, determined no doubt by scientific testing, graphite-shafted irons needed to be longer than their steel brethren. In truth, they were made longer for reasons of manufacturing convenience and expense, which brings us back to the issue of swingweight.

We'll deal with swingweight in more detail below (promise!), but for now I just want to point out that the standard made men's clubs are built with about a D-1 or D-2 swingweight, women's with about a C-5 or C-6 swingweight. Now, as any professional clubmaker will tell you, when the same weight clubhead is built with a lighter-weight shaft, the swingweight will drop like a rock. In other words, the major club companies had three choices. They could: (a) retool and manufacture a second, heavier version of the clubheads for each graphite-shafted model they sold (expensive); (b) add a small weight port to the head and add extra weight to the clubheads when they were assembling them (something that would detract from the cosmetic appearance of the heads the graphic artists insisted); or (c) simply cut the shafts longer, which would make the clubs end up with the same standard swingweight as the steel-shafted version and eliminate the need for making a separate set of heads.

"What the heck," they reasoned. "The average golfer will never notice that extra half-inch, and if they do, just tell 'em that it makes the graphite shafts work better. You know. 'New and improved.' 'Just like the clubs the pros use.' That kind of thing. It sure beats the cost of having to make a different set of heads for graphite-shafted clubs."

I kid you not. That is exactly how decisions like this are made in this crazy industry.

And, if that increased length makes the clubs harder to hit accurately ... well, as we all know: "It's not the arrow; it's the archer."

# Myth #21
# Increasing the swingweight means the club will be heavier.

Okay, *now* we can talk about swingweight. I know I touched on some of this material earlier to make some other points. If so, I am sorry, but it will probably do you good to hear it again as a part of the whole matter of the "swing feel" of your clubs.

Let's start with the statement that increasing a club's swingweight means the club will be heavier. It's not true, at least not to any significant extent. A club's total weight and swingweight are two very different things, and you need to be aware of the difference.

There are two ways to weigh a golf club. The first is the obvious one. You take a golf club, put it on a scale, and read how many ounces or grams it weighs. That's called the "total weight" of the club. The second is called "swingweight."

Swingweight is not really a "weight" at all. It is the ratio between the weight in the front two-thirds of the club and that in the back one-third. It's really more like a way of expressing the club's "balance" or "swing feel" (i.e., how the total weight of the club is distributed between the clubhead, shaft, and grip).

At one end of the shaft is the clubhead, which weighs a certain amount. At the other end is the grip, which also weighs a certain amount. In between, the shaft itself weighs something. When you grip a club and swing it, the head end has a feeling of heaviness that stands out over and above the weight of the rest of the club. Some clubs feel as though they are very heavy in the head end; others can feel not so heavy. The difference in that feeling among clubs is what the industry calls "swingweight."

Swingweight is not a subjective thing. There really is a way of measuring it. There is a special piece of equipment the golf

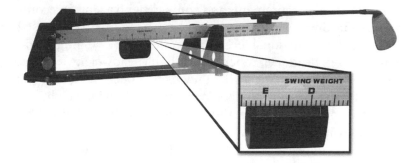

The swingweight scale used by almost every golf club company is designed with the fulcrum point 14 inches from the end of the grip of the club, and with swingweight designations in letter and number increments, i.e., C-6, D-2, E-4, etc.

industry has been using since the 1920s to measure swingweight. This device allows companies and people who build clubs to know how to assemble them to achieve a specific swingweight goal. The industry calls it a scale because it measures a factor that most like to think of as a form of a weight.

The grip end of a club is secured against the end of the swingweight scale (see figure above), and the "teeter-totter" where it rocks up and down ( i.e., the scale's fulcrum) is 14 inches down from the end of the grip. A weight can be moved back and forth along the beam of the scale until the club is balanced. This slide weight will point to a letter-number designation such as C-6, D-2, or E-4. *That* is the swingweight measurement for that club.

The lower the letter-number combination, the lighter the head will feel when you swing the club. The higher the letter-number reading, the heavier it will feel. Ninety-nine percent of the men's clubs coming from the factory are swingweighted either D-1 or D-2. Most women's clubs are built with a lower swingweight in the middle-to-high C range. And the rule of thumb is that *all* the clubs in the set should be built to the same swingweight except the sand and lob wedges, which will usually be built to a higher swingweight than the numbered irons and PW.

Finally, there is no specific way of determining what swingweight is correct for any golfer, at least not in the way you can, for example, take measurements and come up with a length recommendation. Swingweight has always been a judgment call, based on the golfer's individual feel. Some golfers like swinging a club with a heavy head feel, others like a light headweight feel, but most golfers have no idea what they like … because no one has ever bothered to explain to them what the heck swingweight was or why it could be important to the performance of their clubs.

That's why we wrote this book.

As for swingweight selection, it all boils down to this. The stronger you are physically and/or the more downswing force you apply, the higher you will *probably* want your club's swingweight to be. I say "probably" because the only way you will know for sure is to work it out with a qualified custom clubmaker. It's a cinch that the answer will not be found in the neon and chrome of your local big box golf store … yeah the one over by the freeway.

# Myth #22
# The clubs sold in the pro shops and big golf stores are the best clubs for my game.

As a golf club designer who has designed hundreds of different models during the 30-plus years I have been in the golf business, I can tell you that the quality of the clubheads, shafts, and grips created by the big, heavily marketed golf companies is actually very good. They might not be the right clubheads, shafts, and grips for the majority of golfers, but their technical quality is outstanding.

The reason they might not be right for *you*, however, is that these companies ruin all their hard design work by selling their clubs under a single set of "average" specifications. Unfortunately, the specifications they choose might allow (maybe) 10 percent of all golfers to play to the best of their abilities. As for the rest of you ... Hey, these are just like the clubs the pros use!

Why don't these golf companies do what the bat and racket makers do and build their clubs to a variety of specifications, so golfers of all different sizes, strengths, athletic abilities, and swing characteristics can buy the right clubs off the rack and head out to the course to play?

They can't, because if they did, they would go out of business. They would have to manage thousands of product options instead of ten or twenty. And, even if the golf companies could somehow manage their inventory, the retailers who sell the clubs to the golfers would never, ever, agree to stock all those different combinations, or else *they* would go bankrupt.

I'm sure at one point or another you've been in a big box retail golf store, and I'd like you to think for a moment about what you saw. My guess is that you saw eight to ten brands of golf clubs, with each brand having two to four different models. The only "fitting option" you might have seen among those brands and models would have been a handful of driver lofts and maybe two or three shaft flexes. Never mind that there are not enough driver loft options to properly fit most golfers, and no standard exists for what constitutes any given shaft flex.

If you know anything about the retail business, you know that stocking eight brands times two models each, times a minimum of eight different fitting options, times three to six required variations per fitting option, is nearly impossible. It would require stocking a minimum of over seven hundred unique sets in each store! Your accountant and banker would quickly tell you not to touch that deal with a ten-foot pole, or else you'll be headed for Chapter 11. In a nutshell, even if a golf company *wanted* to offer a wide variety of custom fitting options to be sold off the rack, *it simply can't!*

As a result, as the golf industry has grown over the years, companies have resorted to offering golf clubs made to one standard length, loft, lie, face angle, shaft weight, swingweight, and grip size. In each model of each brand, you will see only a handful of driver lofts, and a choice of two or three shaft flexes (and neither you nor the golf sales people have any idea how stiff they really are).

Don't you think it's a little weird that almost no one asks, "if bats and rackets are commonly stocked and sold in all their necessary fitting options, why aren't golf clubs?" The few people who might have thought about it enough to ask are typically told: "Custom fitting is only for *good* golfers," or "Custom fitting? Sure, we do that. Here, hit a few balls at our indoor net and tell me which club you like," or, "Golf is a hard game, and someday when you improve your swing, you'll hit these clubs better." *It's like it is somehow your fault that you don't see lower scores after buying a set of clubs that were never designed for your use in the first place.*

So exactly what is it about standard off-the-rack clubs that keeps you from playing your best? That's a good question, and one that you need to ask, since gazillions of golfers have been buying these clubs for decades, thinking everything's fine.

- Drivers and fairway wood lengths are too long for at least 80 percent of all golfers, which prevents them from hitting as far or as accurately as they could.
- 3-woods are made with too little loft for the vast majority of golfers to hit high enough reach their maximum potential distance.
- Few off-the-rack drivers are made with the face angle options necessary to allow golfers who slice or hook the ball to reduce their problem.
- Few companies offer their drivers with the loft options necessary to allow golfers with an average- to lower-than-average swing speed to maximize his or her distance.
- To keep their inventory units manageable, almost every big golf company gives golfers only one weight option in their shafts. This, in turn, makes it almost impossible for the golfer to match the total weight and shaft stiffness to his or her strength and swing tempo.
- Off-the-rack clubs are made to only one swingweight for men and one for women, which also makes it impossible for the golfer to match the headweight feel of the clubs to his or her strength and swing tempo.
- With no standards for flex in the industry, it is impossible for golfers to know whether the clubs they buy off the rack will have the right flex for their swing speeds and their downswing force.
- Off-the-rack clubs are offered in one—and only one—lie angle, yet the differences in golfer height, arm length, stance posture, and position at impact are vast.
- Little, if any, attention is paid to set makeup. Handing you a set composed of 1-, 3-, and 5-woods and 3-iron through pitching wedge, with a sand wedge thrown in, is much easier. It also prevents the retailers from having to deal with "broken-up sets."

This off-the-rack mentality winds up extending to other areas as well. For example, how many golfers are even asked about the size of their hands, so that at least the right size grips could be applied? Changing grips is simple, fast, and cheap, and any store could do it, but when do you see even *that* fitted to the individual golfer?

Granted, there are more earth-shaking problems in the world, but within the sphere of this great game—a game that is enjoyed by millions upon millions of people around the world—you're definitely not being treated the way you should.

But as I said, and I do mean it, the standard made clubheads, shafts, and grips are very well engineered and made. You just don't want to actually use them in their off-the-rack form.

# Myth #23

# The more expensive the club or the shaft, the better it will perform.

There is an old saying—everyone's heard it—that goes: "You get what you pay for." Well, in golf that's not necessarily true. In golf "You get what you ask for ..." No, let me rephrase that. "You get what you *demand.*" And that can only happen if you know what you *need.*

When my writing partner, Tom Grundner, and I first started doing these books, we had to submit something called a book proposal. A part of that is a section in which we had to list the competition that was out there for the book we were proposing. You might be astonished to learn that there was none. Prior to Tom's and my book *The Search for the Perfect Golf Club* in 2005, no one had ever written a book that explained to the average golfer how golf clubs really worked! Of the very few equipment-related books that had been written, all were done by magazine writers with no training or experience in designing or fitting golf clubs.

As I mentioned in the introduction, most golfers do not know much more about golf clubs than what they read in golf magazine advertisements, or see in TV infomercials. That is an unbelievable shame. I don't believe it has a parallel, at least not to this extent, in any other sport.

You say you can read about golf clubs in the various golf magazines? Yes, you can, but stop for a moment to think about what you're reading. How do golf magazines stay in business? Money from advertisements, right? Now think about who's buying those ads—to the tune of $20,000 to $70,000 per page, with multiple pages from each advertiser being common over the twelve issues each year.

Sure, the golf magazines book a lot of ads from companies that sell cars, software, electronics, liquor, watches, and any other product that has an appeal to the golfing demographic. But they also sell even more ads to the companies who, yes, you guessed it, offer the standard made golf clubs that I am criticizing.

As a designer who can occasionally construct a sentence, I have "written on the side" or "advised" the equipment writers for just about every golf publication in the past thirty years. From this experience I can tell you that each equipment writer routinely gets an earful from the marketing executives of just about every golf club company, complaining that the magazine did not write enough, or write positively enough, about the company's club models. It is not uncommon for these marketing people to threaten a diversion of ad dollars from the magazine unless "appropriate attention" is paid to the company's golf clubs in print.

Now let me ask you another question. How often have you ever read in a golf magazine about *professional* custom fitting? How about reading that the woods you're buying are longer than even the pros would dare to play, or that your new 5-iron has the same loft as yesterday's 3-iron? I scan the golf magazines regularly, and I can assure you no golf magazine would ever say anything critical or in opposition to one of their advertisers' interests unless they were getting ready to change the focus of the publication from golf to something new ... like maybe computers!

As a result, millions of golfers are indeed getting what they pay for, but what they're paying for might bear no resemblance to what they actually *need* to play the game better and enjoy it more.

You say you just paid $400 for a driver? Great. After all, it must be a good one—it cost enough. And you might be right, but you will *only* be right if that club has a length, loft, shaft flex, and other factors that *fit your size, strength, athletic ability, and swing characteristics*. If it doesn't, practically any professional clubmaker in the country could build you a driver that will run circles around that one for less than $400. So ... did you get what you paid for?

At this writing there is, I kid you not, a *single* graphite shaft on the market that sells for *one thousand* dollars! The thinking of these companies seems to be that "if someone is dumb enough to pay that kind of money for one of these shafts, then we'll sell it to them." It would be laughable if it weren't for the fact that that kind of cynical philosophy has come to underlie much of the golf industry these days.

The performance and feel of a graphite shaft is determined by its specific weight, its overall stiffness design, its torque, and how its weight is distributed over the length of the shaft. Yes, there are many different graphite raw materials with an accompanying range of costs. And yes, it is quite possible to make two shafts with the same characteristics using graphite raw materials that differ hugely in price.

But I'll let you in on something. Any two shafts that have the same characteristics (weight, stiffness, torque, and weight distribution) *will perform exactly the same*. So, for Pete's sake, if you're custom fitted into two shafts that perform the same for your swing, buy whichever shaft is cheaper! Trust me, you are getting nothing additional by paying a higher price. Now, use the money that I just saved you to take your "significant other" out for a nice dinner, OK?

If it sounds like I am blaming you for spending $400 on a standard made driver or $300 for that "new shaft that everyone's talking about," trust me, I am not. How were *you* supposed to know that a 9-degree driver requires a 110 mph swing speed to be most effective? How were *you* supposed to know that a 46-inch shaft is nigh on uncontrollable in the hands of the average golfer? How were *you* supposed to know that the flex marking on your shaft was meaningless? How were *you* supposed to know, when the people who should have told you those things, didn't?

You get what you pay for? Yes, that's true, if you know *what* to pay for.

I'll have a lot more to say about all this in the last section of the book, "A Few Final Thoughts." But for now, let's go on and see what else you were not told.

# Myth #24

# A proper set of clubs consists of 1-, 3-, 5-woods, 3–9 irons, pitching wedge, sand wedge, and putter.

When you walk into the average golf store or pro shop, you will typically see a glittering array of club sets laid out before you. There will be all sorts of brand names, head sizes, shapes, and colors. But the one thing they will almost always have in common is their composition, known in the world of custom clubmaking as the "set makeup." Full sets typically consist of three woods (driver, 3-wood, 5-wood), eight irons (3 through pitching wedge), a sand wedge, and a putter, and that's what the majority of golfers will buy.

Now, given that, may I ask a simple question?

Why?

I mean … why that set makeup? Did some golf god come down from Mount Augusta with a mashie in his (or her) hand and decree that it must be thus? No. A marketing department somewhere in a chrome-and-glass conference room, with input from the purchasing manager and accounting staff, decreed that set composition. After all, the less deviation from the mass production formula, the lower the overall costs and the higher the profits. As you have learned in this book, this is the same corporate team that over the years has given you:

- Drivers with a length that is too long and lofts that are too low for your swing speed, which reduces your distance,
- A "required" 3-wood that has too little loft for you to be able to get the ball off the deck and well up in the air,

- Irons with increased lengths and lowered lofts so that, now, at least two clubs have become unusable for most golfers,
- Oversized heads that don't inherently add anything to the average golfer's game,
- The same lie angle for golfers who range in stature, setup, and swing from petite to gorilla,
- And, mystery shaft flexes that don't allow you to know whether they are appropriate for your game or not.

Other than that, they are a fountain of wisdom for the golfer.

The USGA says you cannot have more than 14 clubs in your bag. Fortunately, they don't tell you *which* 14 clubs you can carry. Fine, then let's go through a typical set and ask a few questions about what might be the best buy for *you*—not some marketing department or their big box retail golf store partners.

Perhaps we should start with the driver and ask: why do you have one? I know … you're *supposed* to have one—at least that's what you've been told. And it's true; the driver is an extremely useful club for achieving your maximum possible distance off the tee—if you have a driver that will legitimately allow you to do that.

But let's assume you have an average adult male swing speed of say 87 mph (we'll round it off to 90). To get maximum distance off the tee (which is the whole point of a driver, right?) you would need a loft of about 13 degrees. Now look at the loft of your driver. Does it say 13 or 14? If so, please pass the word to all your friends who share an average to lower-than-average swing speed as to where you got it, because it's a rare find indeed.

Now look at the loft of your 3-wood. What does *it* say? In all likelihood among today's loft-challenged clubheads it will be close to the 13- or 14-degree range that you need *for a driver*. So why are you spending money on a driver? Why not, instead, get an additional wood? Why not buy a 3-, 5-, 7-wood combination, instead of a 1, 3, 5, and have three woods that you can actually *use*?

How about your irons? The store will want you to buy a set consisting of a 3-iron through pitching wedge, or, since 2006, maybe a 4-iron through gap wedge. But, before you do that, I'd like to ask you another question.

Seriously, how consistently well do you hit the 3-, 4-, and even today's loft-challenged, modern 5-iron? If you are like most golfers the answer is: not that well and certainly not consistently solidly and high. So, why are you buying them? Why not instead replace them with clubs that you stand a chance of actually using? I am speaking here, of course, of hybrids.

Hybrids are essentially easier-to-hit substitutes for the long irons, including the 5- and sometimes even the 6-iron. They have become necessary because the traditional long irons, and even middle irons, have become unhittable for many golfers because of the vanishing loft disease we described in Myth #1. A helpful hybrid should have the same loft and length as the iron it's replacing. In other words, it should have the shot distance of a low-lofted iron, but, because the center of gravity has been moved lower and back from the face, it will be easier to hit than its thin-bodied cousin.

All right, so let's say our hypothetical set now consists of a 3-, 5-, and 7-wood, and 3-, 4-, and 5-hybrids that have the same length and loft as your hard-to-hit 3-, 4-, and 5-irons. That's six clubs. We still need to locate eight more.

The shorter irons are probably okay to put in your bag. That would be 6-iron through 9-iron. But do be careful with that 6-iron. If your consistency ratio for the 6-iron is less than two-thirds, meaning you only hit the 6-iron solid and high two-thirds of the time, go with the 6-hybrid.

Okay, so now we have ten clubs—four to go. Let's talk about wedges.

You will have room in your 14-club bag for three wedges because you have to leave room for the putter. Two of them are no-brainers, the pitching wedge and the sand wedge, and one is not. We referred to it earlier; it's called a "gap wedge."

The pitching wedge will probably come with your set of irons. It's needed to produce short, accurate approach/chip-'n'-run shots to the green. The sand wedge is, of course, needed for those days when your round of golf seems more like a trip to the beach or a jungle safari.

The gap wedge is a club with a loft that is about halfway between those of your pitching wedge and your sand wedge. In other words, if your sand wedge is 56 degrees and your pitching wedge is 48 degrees, your gap wedge would split the difference—52 degrees. As we discussed in Myth #1, all of your irons, again because of the vanishing loft disease, have moved up and away from your sand wedge. That creates a gap between the pitching and sand wedges that must now be filled, or else you'll be continually trying to overhit your sand wedge to reach distances in between.

If you want to add a lob wedge with 60 degrees of loft, you can always drop the 3-hybrid to make room for it within the rule of 14 clubs. Most golfers hit their 7-wood and 3-iron/hybrid close to the same distance anyway.

The last club in your set is the putter, but *please* do not take this club lightly. Of all the clubs that should be custom fitted—and all of them should be—this one has the highest priority. Whether you are a novice or a tour pro, the putter is the club that you will use more than any other in your set. It's the club that most directly impacts your score. It is so important that we have an entire book about putters (and wedges) that will be coming out soon. Please select this club with care and make sure the lie angle, length, and loft of the putter truly fit your stance, posture, and manner of stroke.

One other brief comment.

If you are a senior or especially a female golfer you might sometimes feel sales pressure to go with graphite shafts in your irons instead of steel. You will be told that graphite shafts are lighter (which is true) and thus more suited to the senior or female golfer (which is not necessarily true, depending on your strength and athletic ability). If you feel like you really *do* need the lightest possible clubs, then by all means get the graphite shafts. If not—if the slight difference in weight will probably make no significant difference to your game—then go with lightweight steel shafts. They are less expensive and will work just as well, as long as you have an experienced clubmaker with good shaft knowledge helping you.

So now we have our set. It consists of: 3-, 5-, and 7-woods, 3-, 4-, and 5-hybrids, 6-, 7-, 8-, and 9-irons, three wedges (pitching, gap, and sand) and a putter. Fourteen clubs. Is that the set for you? Well, maybe—and maybe not.

I've made a lot of assumptions about your game in formulating this hypothetical set. Those assumptions might, or might not, be applicable to you.

This gets us back to the topic of having your clubs custom tailored—the same way you would for a suit of clothes. The only way you can know for sure whether this is the right set for you, and specifically what each club should be like, is to see your "tailor" — your local independent professional clubmaker. Sorry, folks, but until golf retail stores start having qualified clubmakers on premises or at least on call, and allowing them to take the time necessary to come up with each golfer's very best set of custom fitting recommendations, that's the only way to do it.

He or she will steer you in the right direction—that's all part of the job; and as with a good tailor, it's how a custom clubmaker stays in business.

# Fitting

# Myth #25

# I was "custom fitted" at the driving range (or retail golf store, or pro shop).

Well, maybe you were and maybe you weren't. The problem is that there are so many definitions of what constitutes "custom fitted golf clubs" or a "custom fitting session." One of my colleagues in the clubmaking business perhaps described it best when he used the analogy of a car wash.

Let's say your car is looking pretty trashed out. At one level, you can hose your car down with water and squirt off the worst of the dirt. That's an improvement. Not great, but better than nothing. At the next level, you can get out the bucket and soap and give the car a good scrubbing. That's even more of an improvement. Or you can pull out all the stops and scrub it, rub it out, wax it, and detail it inside and out. Now you're ready for show time. The point here is that each of the above can be described as "getting the car washed."

Getting custom fitted for golf clubs is much the same. There are several levels, and all can (and have) been described with the words "custom fitted clubs." Since a lot of club companies and golf equipment retailers are becoming aware that custom fitting is now "in," golfers are going to be seeing that phrase a lot. That's why it's really important for golfers to know what is and is not a real custom fitting session. Here's a quick summary.

**Level One (The UNfitting):** Believe it or not, there are some who feel that hitting a few shots with provided clubs at a driving range during a trial-and-error "Demo Day" is an exercise in custom fitting. Wrong. While it sounds good to "try before you buy," Demo Days are in no way a custom fitting, because no effort is being made to try to customize the clubs being hit to the individual size, strength, athletic ability, and swing mechanics of the individual golfer.

**Level Two (The "Is That All?" Fitting):** A number of golf companies have created neat fitting carts filled with clubs whose lot in life is to sit patiently on the driving range until someone comes over and pays attention to them. Frankly, the vast majority of fitting carts are created to "fit" irons to men, but only in the company's one or maybe two iron models, which are shafted with one model of shaft, in a couple of different flexes. Rarely will you see a "ladies' flex," (whatever that means—see Myth #31) on one of those carts. If you do, there will only be one "maybe it's an L, maybe it's not" flex in one model of a women's shaft as opposed to "maybe it's an A, R, or S, maybe it's not" in only one model of shaft for the men.

What's missing when you subject yourself to a "cart fitting" are the following: (1) a wider selection of ironhead models; (2) a wider selection of shaft models in different weights, shaft bend profiles, and flexes; (3) a proper means of identifying the correct length for the golfer outside of the "here, try this" approach; (4) the proper swingweight or club moment of inertia to match a golfer's unique strength, swing tempo, and athletic ability; and (5) the most comfortable grip model and size.

Oh, did I forget the woods in this cart fitting?

Those that include woods also fall well short of offering the golfer the full complement of fitting specifications that you would find in a real custom fitting session. Which fitting specifications are missing? How about: enough loft angle (and any face angle) options to maximize your distance and correct misdirection problems; a wider variety of shafts in different weights, bend profiles, and flexes; short enough lengths to satisfy the vast majority of golfers; and a variety of swingweights, not to mention a variety of grip types and sizes. (And no, not every lady golfer should be using a "ladies' grip.")

**Level Three (The "I *Think* I Had a Custom Fitting" Fitting):** Many golfers would consider hitting shots on a launch monitor at a retail golf store to be a higher level of fitting. And they'd be right as long as: (a) the operator of the launch monitor really knew how to translate the results into accurate fitting specifications; (b) the fitting session lasted at least thirty to forty-five minutes and included several other measurements and analyses; and (c) the clubs they fit you with required you to come back another day to pick them up, because alterations or new assembly of the clubs had to be done.

If your fitting session lasted twenty minutes or less and/or if the driver into which you were "fitted" was selected from the store's off-the-rack inventory, you weren't even close to being custom fitted. You were "inventory-convenience" fitted.

The other Level Three fitting that exists is the one that happens via the online questionnaires that some of the well-known standard clubmaking companies offer. I'll be frank about these services. They do a better job of getting you into slightly better clubs than 80 percent of the retail golf stores can. But again, because they don't incorporate any way to see your swing, and they don't ask enough questions to really get to know your unique, individual makeup, your swing characteristics, and your manner of play, they fall way short of presenting you with a complete range of fitting options. This, in turn, makes them fall well short of a Level Four fitting. Someday, someone will come up with a good way to custom fit over the Internet. But believe me, for such a long-distance fitting to be good, it is going to have to include some way to see/measure or otherwise obtain real information about *your swing*.

**Level Four (Now *That* Was a Custom Fitting):** When you enter the world of a Level Four custom fitting, you usually enter the shop of a trained and experienced professional custom club-maker where the focus is on one golfer and one club at a time, not fifteen sets a day sold off the rack. As I've mentioned many times previously, think of it as golf's equivalent of a trip to a custom tailor, but without the high price of a tailored versus an off-the-rack suit.

Prepare to spend at least an hour or more with the clubmaker, as everything from your current set, to your swing, your manner of play, and your priority for improvement is measured, questioned, and analyzed. You'll have a choice of many different shapes, styles, and designs of clubheads, as well as a wide variety of possible shafts and grips, not to mention the myriad of possible length, total weight, and swingweight options from which the clubmaker will choose for you and only you.

In short, your custom set will be built from the ground up to meet all your individual playing and game improvement requirements, not grabbed from something sitting around on the rack. You'll likely have to make at least two and possibly three trips to the clubmaker's workshop, as details are massaged and tweaked into the final individually made product. And you'll be amazed that you won't pay any more than you would for a standard off-the-rack club.

And while I am on the topic of custom clubmakers, please do not assume that all clubmakers are male. There are some superb craftswomen out there, but you have to look for them. Unfortunately, there are not nearly enough female clubmakers in the profession, and that is a situation that needs to change.

# Myth #26

# I can be custom fitted with one of those new interchangeable shaft fitting systems.

In recent years, a number of the big golf companies have begun to offer what they tout as the "ideal" way to be custom fitted to the right driver. The basic idea is to use a mechanical connector that allows you to instantly attach a number of different shafts to their driver heads. You hit the various shafts and come up with the right driver.

Sounds great, doesn't it? Try before you buy, and all that. Unfortunately, it turns out that it's NOT so great. It's not a custom fitting at all. The problem is that it doesn't deal with the things that are so much *more* important in helping you with your game. What you're doing at these sessions is like rearranging deck chairs without addressing the little problem of there being a hole in the side of your ship.

Let's look at the key fitting factors again and go through them one at a time with regard to this new system. I have them in order based on what (for most people) are the most important:

- Length
- Loft
- Face angle
- Swingweight
- Grip size
- and then, for some, the shaft.

The new snap-on system attempts to address the last item on the list, which is also the last thing you probably need to be worried about.

Let's start with length. All the plug-in shafts are going to be made so that the final length of the drivers is the same for each shaft model—namely, the big golf company's "standard driver length," which today is between 45 and 46 inches. As I've pointed out elsewhere in this book, for years the average driver length on the PGA Tour has been 44.5 inches; and if there is any group of golfers who could control a longer length, it would be those pros. Yet, on average, they play with a shorter driver length than what the big golf club companies are expecting *you* to use. In other words—and more to the point of this myth—even the pros would not use a shaft that's as long as the quick-connect shaft you will test.

Then there's loft. Did you test (or even see) a clubhead loft higher than 11 degrees? If your swing speed (with control) is somewhere around 100 mph or more, that 9-, 10-, or 11-degree head will probably be just fine. But the average male golfer swings around 87 mph. To get maximum distance you need a driver with more like 13 degrees. Did you have any of those you could snap on? (Heck, does the company even *make* them?)

How about the face angles? How many options were there for an open, square, or closed face among the heads you looked at? None? Seventy percent of all golfers slice the ball to some degree; and you're saying that the one fitting option that would most likely help them was missing?

And then there's swing weight. Let's say you plug shafts that weigh different amounts—say 55, 65, 75, and 85 grams—into the same head. Unless there is some way to add or change the weight of the head, you're going to end up with a completely different swingweight for each club. So when you made your final selection did you choose the *shaft* that felt the best to you, or did you choose the *swingweight* that felt the best? If it's the latter, then I can save you a lot of money. Just take your old driver in to a club repairperson, and for a few bucks he or she will re-swingweight it.

Grips! I don't know what I can say here that's not covered under Myth #29, but it's very important that you get the right size. Was grip size even mentioned during your snap-on custom fitting session?

And last on the list of important factors is the shaft. Does the shaft make a difference? Sure it does, at least for some people, but, for Pete's sake, it is *not* "the engine that drives the golf club." As for the actual shaft flex of those snap-ons you used, I doubt that even the salesperson knows what it is.

To have a system based solely on shaft testing, to the exclusion of these other factors, and calling *that* "custom fitting" is absurd.

So how could you make this snap-on clubfitting thing work as a genuine technique? You would need to have:

- at least three different clubhead designs, each with a temporary weight port so the snapped-together club can be properly swingweighted before you use it;
- three different face angles for each of the three head designs (open, closed, and square), in at least five lofts (9 to 17 degrees) apiece;
- snap-together shafts of at least three different weights, four different flexes, and five different lengths (42- to the ever-popular 46-inch length);
- and a salesperson who knows what swingweighting is and how to adjust the club.

So that gives us a handy-dandy snap-on clubfitting kit consisting of 105 pieces (the knowledgeable salesperson being optional), and doesn't even get into having a variety of grip sizes on those shafts. Is that pretty much what you saw at the megastore?

The idea of a shaft-to-head connector system for helping to custom fit the driver is sound, but ONLY if you have enough shaft, length, headweight, loft, and face angle variations within the parts you are plugging together. Along with that, you also need store personnel who can guide you toward the options that will most likely benefit you, given your particular swing and game characteristics.

So be careful if you head to the course or store to try out these systems. You need to know that what you'll be experimenting with is *not* covering most of the most critical driver fitting factors.

One last thing before I get off the topic of club-fitting gimmicks.

Have you ever asked yourself why the club companies keep coming up with these various fitting schemes? It's because they *know* that what they're selling you off the shelf is unlikely to be what you actually need to play your best; and they *know* that the only way a golfer can get the right clubs is by having them custom fitted. They also *know* that's not going to happen under the current megastore/fashion boutique retail model that is now in effect.

So what's a company to do? Should they start making more legitimate product choices available? Not a chance—too expensive. Should the retail stores start having professional clubfitters on premises? That desperately needs to happen, but I am not optimistic.

So instead, they have formed the clubfitting-gimmick-of-the-month club. "Hey, mister … look at this! Betcha can't tell which shell the pea is under."

The fact is that a good professional clubmaker is your best source to be fitted for all of the important club specs.

# Myth #27
# Lie angle fitting of the irons is only for good golfers.

If I could wave a magic wand and drill one point into the heads of all golfers, it would be this. *The less skilled you are, the MORE you need equipment that is custom fitted to help compensate for your weaknesses and maximize your strengths.*

Unfortunately, that wand doesn't exist, so that leaves me hunched over a word processor at 11:00 at night. It will have to do.

Let's use the lie angle of your clubs as a perfect case in point.

Have you ever had the experience of making what you thought was a pretty darn good swing, making what you thought was solid contact, and *still* have had the ball sail off into the boondocks? I know, that's the point where you're supposed to shrug, curse the golf gods, and point out to your playing partner for the hundredth time what a tough game it is. But maybe the next time you should take a close look at your club, and ask yourself whether it's fitting you properly.

The whole point of using irons is accuracy, right? I mean, other than at the par-3 holes, you normally don't tee off with them. They're used when you want to place the ball somewhere, either on the green or a specific place on the fairway. So, if I gave you an iron that was intentionally designed to hit crooked, you'd think I was crazy. Yet, in effect, that's exactly what happens when your lie angles are not adjusted to your individual position at impact with the ball.

The lie is the angle between the shaft and the bottom of the clubhead, and, as you move from the low to the higher numbers in the irons, that angle becomes progressively more upright. The objective is to give you clubs whose sole will remain parallel with

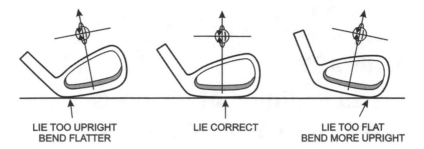

LIE TOO UPRIGHT               LIE CORRECT               LIE TOO FLAT
BEND FLATTER                                            BEND MORE UPRIGHT

the ground when you swing them, even though the shafts are getting progressively shorter.

But here's the kicker—and the thing that most golfers don't know.

If the lie angle is too upright for how you swing, the club will come through with the toe up in the air. When that happens, the loft on the clubhead will cause the ball to go to the left *every time*. It has to, because that's where the face is now pointing, no matter how much you try to line up the bottom of the face to your target. Similarly, if the lie is too flat, the club will come though with the heel up in the air. When that happens, the face will be pointed to the right, and it will hit the ball there—*every time*.

Making matters worse, the higher the loft on the club, the more it will go to the left or right. In fact, lie is usually not an issue with woods because their lofts are much lower than those of the irons. But the irony is that the higher lofted irons are precisely the ones that you choose when you want maximum accuracy.

So, how are your correct lie angles determined? Basically, it starts as a function of your height, your arm length, and your posture over the ball, but the real determination is far more practical than that.

If you're having your clubs tailored for lie, the clubmaker will place a small piece of a special marking tape on the bottom of each iron. He or she will then have you hit a few balls off of a hard-surface mat or plywood board. Each swing will leave a mark on the tape when the sole of your iron makes contact with the mat or board. He'll look at that mark, see how far it is from the center point of the bottom of the iron, and adjust the clubhead's lie angle until your average swing is leaving the mark dead center.

Now, let me ask you something.

Given that golfers come in all sorts of shapes, sizes, and swings, what's the probability that the "one-size-fits-all" lie angles you get on the clubs at the pro shop or local big box golf store are actually going to meet everyone's needs? More importantly, what's the probability that they're going to meet *your* needs?

We've already established that if I were to give you a golf club that intentionally hit the ball crooked you'd think I was crazy. How is it any more sane for you to *buy* one?

# Myth #28
# I can just take my existing clubs and have them custom fitted.

Maybe, but the percentages are not strongly in your favor. Taking off-the-rack clubs and tearing them apart to be retrofitted works only if the things that cannot be changed in the clubs are already perfectly fitted and matched to the golfer's abilities.

So what can't be changed in your current standard made clubs? First, the loft and face angle of your woods. In the old days of wooden woods, a skilled clubmaker could use a file on the face to change the loft and face angle. With every "wood" today being a "metal" there is no way the factory loft and face angle can ever be changed. If you need a different loft to maximize your distance potential or a different face angle to reduce your slice or hook, you have to buy a different driver head with those specifications designed and built into it.

Matching the length of your clubs to your size, athletic ability, and swing is another *extremely important* specification that very likely cannot be changed on your existing clubs, at least unless you can live with numerous strips of lead tape forever residing somewhere on the outside of each head. Since the vast majority of golfers are playing with clubs, especially the woods, that are too long, cutting the end of the shaft to make the clubs shorter is only half of the retrofit requirement. Re-swingweighting the clubs to accompany that shorter length to match *your* strength and swing tempo is critical, or else the shortened clubs won't even come close to having enough headweight feel to prevent you from hitting even more shots off-center and off-line.

The clubheads designed by the big golf companies are all made to weigh the exact amount required to come out to a standard swingweight for the standard length ordained by the company.

For each one inch you might shorten an existing club, 12 grams of weight have to be added back to the head to bring the clubs' swingweight back up to the exact level it was before the length was chopped. Here again, with the old wooden woods, you could remove the metal soleplate, drill a hole in the wood, and pour in lead to re-swingweight the club. With today's metal woods, no such option exists for adding that much weight to get you back to a reasonable, swing tempo–positive, swingweight other than slapping strips of lead tape all over the outside of the clubhead.

If you need a different shaft to match to your swing, such a change can be done on any existing set of clubs. But if the new shaft is of a different weight than the stock, standard model, you still face the problem of "how do I add/remove weight to/from the metal head" to get to the right swingweight for you and for whatever length the new shafts are installed to have.

Ahh, but there is grip size, and yes, that can easily be changed on any existing set of clubs—as long as the new grip weighs the same as the old ones. If the new grip is heavier or lighter, you are facing the matter of re-swingweighting your clubs to get the headweight feel to match your strength and swing.

If getting a new custom built set is not in your financial cards at the moment, then perhaps it might be worth taking them to your local professional clubmaker for a possible retrofitting. Have him or her put you through a fitting analysis to see whether the changes that can help you the most can be done on your existing clubs. Maybe the clubmaker can help, and maybe not. But either way, you'll meet a true craftsman—so that next time you'll know where to go to get clubs that will match every aspect of your individual size, strength, athletic ability, and swing characteristics. Such a set will always be the best and wisest investment in golf clubs you'll ever make.

# Grips and Golf Balls

# Myth #29

## If you slice the ball, use smaller grips; if you hook the ball, use larger ones.

This myth has been around probably for as long as there have been grips on golf clubs. The theory behind it is that if the grips are too large, your wrists will not release in time, and you will block the ball out to the right. If they are too small, you'll get too "wristy" and flick the ball out to the left.

Neither is true for all golfers because each golfer has individual body characteristics and swing techniques. If these things are happening it's probably not because your grips are "too large" or "too small." It's because ... well, I am getting ahead of myself here. I'll explain what's actually happening in a minute.

If there is any part of the golf club that is most often over-looked, it's the grip. Most golfers select grips as an afterthought; we rarely, if ever, clean them; and many people wear them down until they're totally slick and ready to be used to rake cobwebs off the ceiling. Few things about the club are more important, and that's because of one very important point: the grip is the golfer's *only* contact with the club. Yet the grips that come with the standard made clubs in every pro shop and golf store are all one style—one size for men, and one size for women.

One of the golf companies recently conducted an experiment in which a number of golfers were asked to hit five shots in succession with each of three clubs. The clubs were exactly the same in all respects except that one had a brand-new grip on it, the second had a clean but worn grip, and the third was not only worn but had not been cleaned in years (it even had a bit of sunscreen on it). The golfers using the new grip hit the ball an average of seven yards farther than those using the clubs with the worn grip and 13 yards farther than those with the club with the dirty grip and the sunscreen. The reason for these differences is a little villain called centrifugal force.

Centrifugal force is an energy that wants to pull the club out of your hands when you swing it. If you want to experience the feeling of centrifugal force and how it pulls outward on an object, simply tie a weight onto the end of a string and begin swinging the string and the weight around you in a circle. The faster you swing, the more you'll feel the weight on the end trying to pull the string out of your hand.

Well, a golf clubhead on the end of a shaft is like that weight on the end of a string. For a golfer with the swing speed of Tiger Woods (around 130 mph), the centrifugal force with the driver is over 80 pounds, and for the average male golfer (around 85 mph) it will be closer to 50 pounds—all of it trying to yank the club away from you.

The only thing that's keeping that from happening is your hold on the end of the club. Now, if the grip that you've glommed on to is worn, dirty, or the wrong size, the only way you have of keeping the club from flying away is to grip it tighter. And when you grip it tighter you develop what I call "alligator arms." Your forearm muscles tighten up, and any hope of a nice, relaxed, fluid swing is lost.

*That's* where the myth about "If you slice the ball, use smaller grips; if you hook the ball, use larger ones" comes from. Unless your grip is hideously too large or too small, it's because the grip's condition has hosed your swing motion.

So, what are you supposed to do? How are you supposed to pick a grip for your clubs? It all boils down to what feels most comfortable in your hands.

There has been a variety of measurement systems devised to fit you with the right size grip. Some are based on laying your hand over a printed template; some are based on your golf glove size; and some are based on the proximity of the fingertips on your upper grip hand to the base of your hand when you take your grip on the club. None has really proven satisfactory. The reason is that all those measurements go out the window if, when you place the grip in your hand, it still doesn't feel right.

So yes, if you haven't guessed it already, I am advocating that you get custom fitted for grips along with everything else. But, don't panic; it's not that big a deal.

Start by taking your clubs to a place that has a large selection of grips from which to choose. Ideally, they should be mounted on little cut-off pieces of shaft. That's one indication that they are halfway serious about getting your grips right.

Then … I don't know how else to put this, but … fondle the grips. Yes, fondle them. Try to find one whose texture just "feels right" to you. Don't worry about size right now; just worry about texture.

When you find one that you like, ask the salesperson if he or she has a variety of grips in different sizes that you can feel. If he or she hands you a display with a series of identical grips, arranged in size order from one-eighth inch oversize to one sixty-fourth inch undersize, then you've found grip heaven. Fondle them as well. Try to find one whose size just "feels right" to you. Don't worry about texture; just worry about size.

One you've made that determination, hand the clerk the two grips you liked and boldly say: "I'd like this grip, built up with tape to this size, on all my clubs."

If the person says: "Yes, sir. That'll take about a half hour," then you know you've found a store that's a keeper. Do a *lot* of business there, and tell your friends to do their golf club business there too.

If the person looks at you like a deer caught in the headlights of a car, then … well, then you're on your own. Either try some place that has a professional clubmaker on staff, or patiently explain to the sales clerk, "Yes, grips really *do* come in different styles, models, textures, and sizes."

# Myth #30
# There are significant differences among golf balls.

Are there significant differences among golf balls? My answer is a clear and resounding ... yes and no.

Of all the myths presented in this book, this one has perhaps the least clear-cut answer. It's not made obscure because of any technical issues; but rather because it depends on what you mean by "significant" and "differences." (Good Lord, now I am sounding like a politician!)

Let's start with the ways in which all golf balls are the same. That part is easy because they're regulated by the USGA and clearly described.

According to Appendix III to the *USGA Rules of Golf*, the ball cannot weigh more than 1.62 ounces or be smaller than 1.68 inches in diameter, and it has to be round—or at least as round as manufacturing tolerances will allow.

Okay, that's pretty clear. Most golfers are aware of those requirements, but they are not aware of the fine print that follows—and that's where the 1,000-pound gorilla lives.

Besides regulating the golf ball's size, weight, and symmetry, the USGA also regulates how fast it will come off the clubhead (called initial velocity) as well as *how far it will travel*. That's called the Overall Distance Standard. More specifically, the ball had better not come off the face faster than 250 feet per second (with a +2 percent tolerance), or travel farther than 317 yards (with a +3 yards tolerance) when hit by a club traveling at 120 mph (your club speed mileage may vary).

Most golfers, poring through page after page of golf ball advertising promising more distance, have no idea that these limitations exist—and are strictly enforced. If those balls you read about really did provide "more distance," they better not be more than the USGA allows or they would be banned—excuse me, ruled nonconforming—by the USGA. Needless to say, all golf ball makers have their products cinched up to that same standard. They'd be crazy not to.

So, in these respects, all golf balls are the same. They are the same size, the same weight, and the same roundness, and they will not travel farther than a certain distance. So, what's left? Well, two things. The first is the amount of backspin the ball can generate, and the second is something called "feel."

When a golf club strikes a ball, the ball remains connected to the face of the clubhead for less than 0.00047 seconds—that's forty-seven *ten-thousandths* of a second! In that brief period, its velocity off the face, backspin rate, and launch angle are all established. Once the ball leaves the face, the dimples on its surface along with its internal construction further influence its flight. Those dimples, combined with the ball's backspin, affect the airflow around the ball and give it lift, just like an airplane wing.

These things are, of course, well known to the golf ball manufacturers because they provide the basis for their various product lines. Do you want a two-piece with a solid core? Or a multilayered ball? What about the cover? Do you want that in a softer feel or something harder? What compression would you like? And that doesn't even get into variations in the shape, placement, and number of dimples.

Then we get into the variable known as "feel." I have no idea how you can define that—nor does anyone else. That's why the word is a golf marketer's dream.

So then, are there differences among golf balls? There are, but the real question is whether, and to what extent, any of the differences are things that make a difference to your game. To answer *that* question, I will again need to give you a little insight into the golf industry.

As I pointed out under Myth #10, the USGA governs golf play and equipment in the United States and Mexico. They have one huge division that does nothing but monitor and test golf balls and clubs. Their goal is "… to assure that technology does not replace the skill required to play the game." Those are their words, not mine, and they are very good at what they do.

Now, whenever you read about some club or ball that claims it will, by itself, do X for your game, you need to ask: "If that were really true, what's the probability of that technology replacing my skill (or lack thereof) *and* escaping USGA notice?"

The answer in my experience is: none—at least not on any major scale.

"But wait," you might say. "Your whole career—this whole book—is based on making people play better golf through better equipment."

No, that's not true. My whole career and all the books I've written are based on *allowing* people to play better golf through better equipment. There is a difference.

As I said in the introduction, my contention is that the best golf clubs you will ever have are those that are custom tailored to your individual size, strength, athletic ability, and swing characteristics. In other words, the emphasis is on matching the variety of allowable equipment variations to you. *Independent of that specific match, those allowable variations will do nothing, and could even harm your game.*

To bring this back around to our discussion of golf balls: you want a ball that will "hit farther" or travel on a certain kind of trajectory? Fine. Will the current golf balls on the market do those things? I don't know. I assume that, if struck by a robotic hitting machine under certain controlled conditions, they will. But, will they do those things for *you*? Again, I don't know. But I do know this: you will be far more likely to achieve the distance, trajectory, and accuracy you're seeking with clubs that are specifically tailored to you, your swing, and the way you play the game.

As for golf balls, I can only tell you this for certain. They will be a certain size and a certain weight. They will be more or less round, and they will fly only so far—and no farther. They can perhaps offer golfers a little more or a little less backspin, but how much depends on the golfer's swing speed and how he or she swings the clubhead to meet the ball—and that's going to be different for different golfers.

If you consider whatever is left over a "difference that makes a difference," then I guess this item is not a myth.

# Special Populations

# Myth #31
# Women's clubs are designed for women.

What could be more reasonable? You see a set of clubs at your local golf store that's displayed under a sign reading "Women's Clubs." The lettering on the back of the irons is even done in a "tastefully feminine" color, which drives you slightly nuts, but you let it go. What could be more sensible than to assume that these clubs are uniquely designed for women?

Well ... sometimes this is true, but in many (if not most) cases, it is simply not so.

If you don't believe me, ask for or look up the design specs for a set of women's clubheads and compare them with those for a set of men's clubs. In most cases, the very things that need to be modified for women are exactly the same as they are on the men's model. And where things are modified from the men's version, they're not changed enough.

To save you some time, the chart on page 116 is a comparison of the men and women's clubs produced by one of the most recognized golf club companies in the game. And while you're looking at it, check out the men's and women's driver lengths. According to this company, women are supposed to buy drivers that are as long as the average driver length for men on the PGA Tour! (I'll say this much for them, however. You can't really accuse them of false advertising. They did imply in their ads that these were "just like the clubs the pros use," right?)

To get back to my point, the problem is that the vast majority of women golfers need clubs with more loft than what is normally offered. In addition, they need much shorter lengths for all the woods, a set makeup that eliminates the 3- and 4-iron and probably even the 5-iron (thanks to the vanishing loft disease

## Women's Model

| Driver | Lofts Available (degrees) | Length (inches) | Face Angle |
|---|---|---|---|
| | 9 | 44.5 | 1° Closed |
| | 10 | 44.5 | 1° Closed |
| | 11 | 44.5 | 1° Closed |
| | 13 | 44.5 | 2° Closed |

| Irons | Loft | Length |
|---|---|---|
| #2 | 18 | 38.5 |
| #3 | 21 | 38 |
| #4 | 23.5 | 37.5 |
| #5 | 26 | 37 |
| #6 | 29 | 36.5 |
| #7 | 33 | 36 |
| #8 | 37 | 35.5 |
| #9 | 41 | 35 |
| PW | 46 | 34.5 |

## Men's Model

| Driver | Lofts Available (degrees) | Length (inches) | Face Angle |
|---|---|---|---|
| | 9 | 45 | 1° Closed |
| | 10 | 45 | 1° Closed |
| | 11 | 45 | 1° Closed |
| | 13 | 45 | 2° Closed |

| Irons | Loft | Length |
|---|---|---|
| #2 | 18 | 39.5 |
| #3 | 21 | 39 |
| #4 | 23.5 | 38.5 |
| #5 | 26 | 38 |
| #6 | 29 | 37.5 |
| #7 | 33 | 37 |
| #8 | 37 | 36.5 |
| #9 | 41 | 36 |
| PW | 46 | 35.5 |

described under Myth #1), and a choice of at least two different shaft flexes, both of which should be more flexible than any
men's shaft.

I'll use the driver to illustrate what I mean.

The majority of women's drivers are a "ladies' version" of
a men's model, and are cut only one-half to one inch shorter
than the standard 45- and 45.5-inch lengths built for the men.
As I mentioned earlier, the problem is that the men's clubs are
routinely *way* too long. With only a decrease of one-half to one
inch from the standard men's length, the ladies are in even worse
shape then the men when it comes to finding an off-the-rack
driver that will work for them. And it gets worse when you look
at the loft of those drivers.

Rarely are the lofts on the women's drivers higher than the
men's, which means they're not nearly high enough given the
average woman's swing speed. There are hardly any women's
drivers offered with the 15-, 16-, or 17-degree lofts that most
women golfers need to get maximum distance.

Take the chart I just showed you as an example. A lady golfer
would have to have a swing speed of 90 mph or more (LPGA
Tour pros swing at around 97 mph) in order for even the high-
est-lofted driver (13 degrees) to be appropriate. In the absence
of that swing speed—*this company does not make a driver that
is anywhere near what 99 percent of women golfers need*. To be
even more blunt, those 44.5-inch, 9- and 10-degree drivers are
actively *sabotaging* the game of the vast majority of women who
buy them. Yet the set shown here is marketed nationwide, and
thousands of women put their trust in that brand name.

As a result of the above, how many women have found themselves on a tee with a driver they can't control (because it's too
long), and then found that, even when they do connect, the ball
doesn't come close to flying as far as it should (because it's the
wrong loft)?

Worse yet, how many women have quit the game because
they are "just no good at it," not knowing that the fault was not
in their athletic ability but because they were using clubs that
were designed *from the factory* to be essentially unusable in
their hands?

The point here is that there are female, senior, and even some junior golfers who can and should play with the same fitting specifications that you would find in men's clubs. And there are some men who can and should be playing with what are labeled by the golf industry as "senior" or "ladies'" club specifications. The only way to know is to be properly and professionally fitted.

Just because someone put pink, taupe, or mauve paint on their golf clubheads does not mean that they are right for you as a female golfer. Properly fitted golf clubs know no gender restrictions. They only know if they are properly matched to their owner's size, strength, athletic ability, and swing characteristics.

# Myth #32
# Senior golfers need to play with senior clubs.

Really? And which senior clubs might those be? Would they be the ones being swung by a 6-foot, 4-inch retired lumberjack, or are you referring to the ones being used by a 135-pound former bookkeeper? When they start making all senior men in the same size, shape, and athletic ability, the concept of a "senior golf club" will make sense. Until then, the term is a marketing phrase, and nothing more.

Writing about "senior golfers" is very difficult without defining precisely what we mean by that term, so let me try it this way.

For purposes of this discussion, I am defining a senior golfer as any golfer who has reached a point in life where he or she notices a loss of distance or loss of playing skills and attributes that loss to age. Note that this does not necessarily refer to a birth date or the color of anyone's hair, but rather to a time in each golfer's life when he or she begins to lose swing speed, and the backswing gets a little shorter from a loss of body flexibility. That could be at age seventy-five or age forty-five. It depends on the person.

The golf industry tends to use the term "senior golfer" pretty much with a male connotation. Obviously, there are lady golfers who eventually become seniors, but at present the golf industry does not create specific club models for those more seasoned ladies who notice that loss of swing speed and flexibility. From the club company's standpoint, there simply aren't enough of them to represent a viable market, so they just pretend that senior ladies don't play golf. Problem solved.

Off-the-rack senior men's clubs are, like the younger men's clubs, designed for some kind of national average. If you do not fit those parameters, you will be playing with clubs that can't possibly benefit your game. But even if you *do* fit that national average, all might not be well.

Under Myth #12 you learned that the concept of shaft flex has been distorted to the point that it is now meaningless. You've also learned that your off-the-rack options for loft and length aren't much better. So, as a senior golfer, where does that leave you? It leaves you in the same place as every other golfer.

When it comes to golf club selection, commit this to memory: *There is no such thing as a junior, senior, male, or female golfer. There are only golfers with differences in size, strength, athletic abilities, and swing characteristics.* If you somehow buy a set of clubs off the rack that matches *your* specific and highly individual characteristics, it will be a 100 percent pure statistical fluke.

I am fifty-seven years old now, but I have to tell you, I feel just as I did when I used to play tournament golf and compete with other low-handicap juniors, then college players, and after that, fellow PGA club professionals. But my swing speed is 7 mph slower than it was back then, and my backswing is not parallel to the ground anymore. So, sign me up. I am most definitely a "senior golfer" within the definition I just gave.

But I am also a career golf club designer, and I like to think that has had some effect on my personal approach to getting the most from what I presently bring to the tee. Thus, with no trepidation, a few years ago I switched to more flexible shafts in both my irons and woods. Those shafts help me to get more distance and make it easier to get the ball up in the air for my low-trajectory swing tendencies.

I play with a 43.5-inch driver length, although my wrist-to-floor measurement plus the factors of my swing plane and athletic ability suggest it could be 44 to 44.5 inches. Why? Because with my fast downswing tempo I can control the head better with the shorter shaft and heavier clubhead. I hit the ball more consistently on-center, and I can keep the ball on the fairway more often.

The loft of my driver is now 11 degrees, where it was 9.5 ten years ago. Given my reduced swing speed and slightly downward angle of attack my swing creates, I need that higher loft to get maximum distance.

I now carry a 4- and 7-wood where that used to be a 3- and 5-wood. My irons do not include a number lower than 4, and the 4- and 5-irons now happen to be hybrid long iron replacement clubs. Thus my "real irons," all of which have a cavity in the back, start with the 6-iron, where before I was carrying irons from 3 to the wedges.

Because my touch and finesse with my hands is not what it was, I now have a 58-degree sand wedge and a 61-degree lob wedge that I now hit with more of a square setup instead of the wristy, flippy hands that worked so well years ago.

But here's my point. I am *proud* to carry this set makeup, and I don't give a hoot what some other golfer thinks who still has the letter "S" on his shafts.

You see, there is not an off-the-rack "senior set" in the country that would meet my actual needs, and I am by no means a pro. My handicap index is now up to 9.4 since I started my own company, but I know if I tried to play with a set bought off the rack, bought with the knowledge of an average golfer, I'd easily be a 15. As a result, I need my clubs custom tailored even more now as a senior than I did back when I fantasized about being the second coming of Jack Nicklaus. I'd be willing to bet the same thing is true of you as well.

In the final analysis, all we "seniors" can do is play to our strengths—but that's not the same thing as raising a white flag. We might not be able to outhit those young flat-bellies for distance, but we can "out-straight" them off the tee, outthink them on the approach, and positively eat their lunch around and on the greens. You'd be amazed at how satisfying (not to mention profitable) that can be.

If you're interested in playing the best golf you can play, then the game is all about common sense and playing as *smart* as you can play. I mean, if there is anything that a senior golfer should know, it is the old saying: "It's not how, but how many."

# Myth #33

# I can cut down a set for my son or daughter; that's good enough.

Let me put it this way. If you want to make dead certain that your little Tiger or Annika will develop a totally lame swing, all you have to do is cut down a set of adult clubs and give them to him or her. They will be too heavy, too stiff, the wrong loft, the wrong lie, and probably the wrong length. Other than that, they will be just what the kid needs to develop as a golfer.

Should you perhaps cut a club down just to find out if he or she would enjoy taking cuts at a golf ball? Sure, that makes sense, although you might first try to hunt for a single junior club for $5 to $10 at a used sports equipment store. But, when you hear him ask for another bucket or hear her complain about leaving the driving range too soon, it's time to get some proper junior clubs.

Since 2000, there have been a couple of companies that have made a real niche for themselves by offering good quality premade junior sets. The lofts are friendly, shafts are more flexible, weights are a little lighter, and grips are smaller. They offer the sets in premade categories of "age 5–8" and "age 9–12," with the substantial difference being their lengths, which is based on the average heights for kids in these two age groups.

The only drawbacks to the premade junior sets might be their price and the possibility that your son or daughter happens to be outside the national average range of height for his or her age, from which the standard lengths of these sets are created. Thus, we come back to your local professional clubmaker who can custom build him or her (or you) a set. And don't panic about that "custom built" part. It's been my experience that the vast majority of clubmakers do not charge prices for their junior clubs that come even close to the prices you would pay for the premade premium branded junior sets found in retail golf shops. I've found that most custom clubmakers have a real soft spot for kids who are really getting interested in the game.

One last point …

Try to resist the temptation to buy clubs that are too long with the expectation that he or she will "grow into them." A child might well do that, but if they're too long, you're forcing your offspring to hit with something that could cause him or her to learn a bad swing, and you *know* how hard it is to UNlearn that swing later on.

If that means you need to get him or her a new set every year or two, get over it. As long as your kid or grandkid is really into the game, it's a better deal than those tap-dancing lessons you sprang for, not to mention the $200 thin profile/camera/text messaging cell phone he or she just had to have (this month anyway). You're giving the kid a gift that will literally keep giving for the rest of his or her life, long after you're gone. That's no small thing. Besides, it's a small price to pay to watch your son walk up the 18th fairway at Augusta with a 12-stroke lead, or your daughter take that dive into the pond at the Dinah Shore, right?

# Myth #34
# If you are handicapped, you can forget about playing golf.

Boy, is this one ever not true!

There are about 50 million people in the United States with disabilities, and that doesn't count the millions more who have temporary limitations due to an accident or illness. We know that about 10 percent of the general public plays golf, and it is not unreasonable to think that, given the opportunity, about the same percentage of the disabled would also be interested in the game, if given half a chance.

The first problem is how to accommodate the equipment and educational needs of the disabled. The Professional Clubmakers Society (PCS) has formed a Task Force on Fitting the Physically Challenged Golfer to teach clubmakers how to work with this new population and produced a booklet of case studies called *The Forgotten Foursome*. In addition, numerous organizations have been formed for disabled golfers, and the USGA has created a modified version of the Rules of Golf to make the game more equitable for golfers with disabilities.

The second problem is to get the word out to the disabled about these resources and to get them interested in the game. I suspect, however, that it will take little encouragement to get them out on the links, especially those who were avid golfers before their disability.

The third problem is becoming less of a "problem" all the time, and that is providing the modified equipment necessary for the handicapped to play the game.

The equipment needs of this population are as diverse as the disabilities themselves. These disabilities can range from blindness and paralysis, to the loss of one or more limbs, to minor movement and grip restrictions due to arthritis or aging. Even chronic pain in the shoulders, arms, or hands can prohibit a person from playing.

However, a great deal can be done to make the game accessible to golfers with almost any level of disability. The key is to select or create equipment that maximizes comfort and ease of use. And because this is not a domain of any of the golf companies with their standard equipment offerings, it is an area that is strictly handled by the professional local clubmaker who has expanded his or her skills to help such players. For example:

People with joint and tendon injuries can benefit greatly from the new lighter-weight graphite shafts. Shock levels can be greatly reduced from using graphite shafts or by using steel shafts with vibration-dampening systems built in, such as the True Temper Sensicore shafts. You can also use conventional shafts fitted with shock-relief inserts by your local clubmaker.

Grips can be built up or special training grips installed for people who have trouble holding their clubs while they swing. Arthritis will do that to you. You can also get special golf gloves with leather loops that will hold the club to your hand when your grip can't.

Almost everyone will experience decreased flexibility and strength as they get older, and this will translate into a loss of distance. The usual instant fix for distance loss is to increase club length. The problem, as we have seen above, is that the longer the club, the harder it is to control. This is especially true of drivers, and especially true for persons with disabilities.

But, there *is* another trick left in the bag. Don't increase the length of the woods; decrease the loft of the mid-to-short irons. By slightly decreasing the loft of, say, the 5- or 6-iron through the wedges, you get increased distance on the second shot without running the risk of total insanity off the tee.

There are other things that can be done.

Golfers who have lost flexibility can often benefit by having a light total weight but high swingweight clubs. This helps them to better feel where the club is located in space as they deliver the swing. Furthermore, they are likely to benefit from a more flexible shaft.

Even the lack of mobility has been overcome. Almost all public and most private courses are now barrier-free. The person who is wheelchair-bound or who uses a cane or walker now has access to the course. There are even specially designed golf carts with seats that tilt out and swivel to allow a "turn through the ball," so even the paraplegic golfer can still play.

As more and more of this kind of equipment becomes available, the more handicapped golfers will be showing up on our courses.

They are ready to play.

# The Golf Industry

# Myth #35
# My clubs are just like the ones the pros use.

Not ... on ... your ... life.

The clubs you buy in the retail stores are to the clubs the pros use as the Chevrolet Monte Carlo in your driveway is to the one Jeff Gordon drives in NASCAR races. I'll use a set of Payne Stewart's clubs as an example, and trust me, this process is no different for any pro on any pro tour.

In 1999, I had the pleasure of designing what tragically turned out to be the last set of clubs Payne Stewart played in competition. His set required four separate visits to my workshop over the course of six months.

Payne had just concluded a contract with Spalding that required him to play the company's investment-cast cavity-back irons, but he was most eager to get back to playing with a forged carbon-steel design. I kept spare "raw forgings" from a set that I had earlier designed for just such projects as Payne's.

Payne's first visit aimed toward finding out what he liked to see in the various irons as he set up behind the ball. This would include things like leading edge shape, top-line thickness, toe shape, toe transition, offset, and many other subtle areas of head design. Between visits one and two, I ground, filed, bent, and formed Payne's preferences into each head in the set.

During visit number two, Payne stood right next to me as I worked each head into a nearly final form. Payne would then insert a shaft in each head, assume an address position, look, look again, scratch his head, and, in whatever way he could, express what was good, bad, or indifferent about each one. From this, I now had a much clearer picture of what he wanted and could final-grind each head after he left. Matters like center-of-gravity positions were my responsibility to manipulate according to the ball flight trajectory wishes that Payne had expressed.

During the third and fourth visits, the still not completely finished heads were assembled with different shaft options. Payne hit shot after shot with each club, commenting only when he felt it appropriate to clarify his desires for the feel of both the club-head and the shaft during the shots. Only when Payne gave final approval to each club was his job completed, and mine shifted into another gear.

All tour players in both the PGA and LPGA require a minimum of two identical sets of clubs, one to travel with and one to keep in a safe place, packed and ready to ship. Should the nightmare scenario occur—of their clubs being lost or even stolen—they can obtain a duplicate of the old set literally overnight. Because of that requirement, I also had to make templates for each head profile along with all sorts of measurements and photographs that would allow me to remake the backup set completely from scratch without having any of the original clubs to guide me.

In total, I probably spent somewhere in the area of three hundred hours from start to finish on the two identical sets. It's something you should keep in mind the next time you see an ad implying you will be playing clubs "just like the ones the pros use." Trust me. You won't.

# Myth #36
# Any club that is not a "brand name" is junk.

Whoa, some real reeducation is in order here, because among those "unknown" brands you just wrote off are some of the world's finest golf club heads. On the other hand, some of them would be better candidates for a landfill than your golf bag. I want to give you a bit more insight into the golf club business, but first I need to make a couple of crucial distinctions.

If by a non-brand name you mean what some people call "clones," then that's something else entirely. Cloning occurs when an unscrupulous company makes models that copy every detail of a heavily marketed clubhead, right down to coining a name that might even phonetically sound like the model name of the original design. Those heads are often in violation of patent or trademark laws, and most club companies will vigorously prosecute the people who make them—and sometimes even the people who *buy* them.

There are also clubs that are known as "knock-offs." These are heads that are similar to better-known clubs but do not violate any patents. They are not illegal, but they are also usually not very good either. Low-quality foundries that are not skilled enough in their production operations to attract business from serious quality-minded golf companies usually make such knockoff heads. They are, in turn, sold by even lower-quality companies who market them to golfers who think that "close enough is good enough."

Lofts, lies, and head weights are usually far outside the tight production tolerances delivered by the quality foundries. To save money, the metal is often a mixture of re-melted scrap with a bit of new material thrown in. These companies and their customers

damage the reputation of all the quality-minded component
manufacturers because most golfers lump every one of the component companies together into one barrel of bad apples.

But there is also a third category of company that you would
do well to take very seriously.

You are certainly aware of the major golf club companies—you
routinely see their names on the pages of the golf magazines or on
the bags, caps, and visors carried and worn by the pros. What you
might not know, however, is that while those companies might
*assemble* their clubs, they do not actually *manufacture* anything.
Everything they sell—heads, shafts, grips—is made by someone
else, somewhere else. Take clubheads, for example.

Virtually no golf clubheads are made in the United States anymore. Well over 90 percent of them are made in either Taiwan
or mainland China. That means that the number of foundries
capable of producing high-quality golf clubheads is finite; there
are maybe ten or twelve in the world. *Every* reputable golf club
company has its heads made at one (or more) of those foundries.
Whether you are talking Callaway, Titleist, or Ping, or whether
you are talking about my company, Tom Wishon Golf Technology, *the heads come from the same manufacturing foundries*. The
same people, using the same materials, to the same standards,
on the same machines, make them.

There are two factors that separate the elite from the common
in this business. The first is the quality of design. The finest head
designs in the world do *not* necessarily come from brand-name,
mass-advertised, mass-marketed companies. The second factor
is the care and skill with which the club is put together, *custom
tailored to your specific needs*; and, that is where the brand names,
inherently, cannot compete. Well-engineered clubhead, shaft, and
grip designs, when professionally custom fitted, are not made one
hundred thousand at a time to the same specifications. They are
made *one* at a time, to *your* specifications. They are not "one size
fits all"; they are "one club, one customer, one clubmaker."

You would not automatically equate a large advertising budget with quality in any other area in which you have significant
knowledge. Don't do it with golf.

# And the Mother of All Myths . . .

# Myth #37

# I am not a good enough golfer to be custom fitted—besides, it's not the arrow, it's the archer.

Nope! As I've tried to point out throughout this book, the truth is exactly the reverse of that.

Okay, I know what you're thinking. "That's interesting and all that, but, what the heck, a club is a club. It's not the arrow; it's the archer. It's not the equipment that makes a good golfer."

Really? Have you ever tried shooting a bow with a bent arrow?

Let me put it another way. Imagine, if you will, a track meet. Three sprinters are in the blocks at the starting line. All are trained athletes; all have worked for years developing their abilities. But the first runner is wearing grossly oversized combat boots; the second is wearing street shoes that are way too tight for him; and the third is wearing perfectly fitted, state-of-the-art track shoes.

Who do you think is probably going to win the race?

Sure, it's possible that runners one or two might win by virtue of a talent that simply overpowers the limitations of their equipment. But would you call it a fair race? Would you say: "It's not the shoes, it's the runner"? I doubt it. And if you wouldn't say it of that hypothetical track meet, why would you say it about golf?

Now, let's be clear—I am *not* saying you can *buy* skill as a golfer. I am not saying that by spending enough money, you can somehow go from being a total duffer to qualifying for next year's U.S. Open. Buying new clubs—even truly custom built ones—is *not* a substitute for learning and "grooving" the proper swing fundamentals. Never has been. Never will be.

I *am* saying, however, that equipment that doesn't fit—that's the wrong length, or flex, or design—can keep you from being all that you *could* be as a golfer, and it might even keep you from becoming a golfer at all. Simply put, understanding how golf clubs work and adjusting your clubs to fit your own size, strength, athletic ability, and swing characteristics will make you a better player. When you play better, you will enjoy the game more, and ultimately that's what it's all about, isn't it?

To get back to our myth, the pros and very low-handicap golfers—male or female—are skilled enough to be able to play well with almost any club. You, on the other hand, are not; which means *you* need properly fitted golf clubs even more than *they* do. You see, the pros know that to play their best, they need to have their clubs custom tailored to minimize their particular swing errors and maximize their swing strengths. Does that sound like something you somehow *don't* need?

The idea of custom fitting is to have clubs in which the individual design characteristics of the clubhead, shaft, and grip are matched to your size, strength, athletic ability, and, most of all, your swing characteristics. Further, they are custom assembled to allow you to maintain essentially the same swing throughout the set, yet give predictably different distance and trajectory results. And true custom fitted clubs, in most cases, do not cost more than what you would pay for standard-made clubs off the rack.

This is the essence of clubmaking and design. Unfortunately, it almost never happens because so few golfers ever do more in their search for their perfect golf clubs than drive to the local golf store or click on their computers.

The average golfer could drop six to eight strokes by simply realizing that the golf club is not a "club." *It is not something to which you need to adjust—it is something that needs to be adjusted to you.* It really *is* a superbly designed, surgical-quality instrument—if you take the time to discover how it can be fitted to complement your swing. The idea here is to play the game with one swing and 14 controlled results—not 14 swings and 144 prayers.

Yes, it's true, golf is inherently a difficult and often frustrating game, but that's part of its charm, part of the fun. As with any game, however, if poor equipment rigs the game so you can't possibly win, suddenly it becomes a whole lot less charming and not fun at all.

# A Brief Word about Custom
# Clubmakers and How to Find Them

Throughout this book I have been harping on the theme: "Get thee to a professional custom clubmaker." That's fine, but how does the average golfer know where to go and who's good at what they do? Unfortunately, the answer is not a simple one.

Custom clubmaking has been around for over five hundred years, but the idea of going to a pro shop or retail golf store to buy golf clubs did not originate until the early 1900s. Before that, if you wanted to buy a set of clubs, you *had* to find a custom clubmaker who would build the clubs one at a time, to your specifications, just as their modern counterparts do today.

But by the early twentieth century the game was growing rapidly, and clubmakers wanted to find a way to increase their business to meet this growth in demand. The solution was to put their clubs on display in places where golfers naturally congregate, such as golf courses and pro shops. From there it was only a small step for these individuals to form companies and develop relationships with hosts of retailers. While this became an efficient way of distributing large numbers of clubs quickly, it resulted in the demise of the "one club–one customer–one clubmaker" concept. In its place we've got today's model of selling standardized one-size-fits-all clubs off the rack. It was simply a matter of economics. From a pure business standpoint, you can't go from hundreds of millions to more than a billion dollars in sales by custom fitting golfers one at a time—and that's where the golf club industry is today.

Nevertheless, professional custom clubmaking still exists as a profession, but it's not one that's widely understood. Most golfers vaguely know that custom clubmaking is out there, but it's not the first option that springs to mind when they're looking for clubs. And please ... do not confuse the custom fitting programs of the big golf companies with true tailoring of clubs to each individual golfer's swing. The profession of golf clubmaking—one set, one golfer, at a time—is so small compared to the massive business of selling standard made clubs, that it gets drowned out.

Custom clubmaking began to revive itself in the 1970s, when a trend emerged among pros and low-handicap amateurs to play the game with refurbished wooden woods and forged irons originally made in the 1930s to 1960s. Good golfers were not impressed by the golf industry's move into cast stainless steel heads; and they insisted that the old, classic, wooden woods and forged carbon steel irons, refurbished with modern shafts and grips, were the best clubs with which to play. Given that demand, someone had to install the new shafts and grips, and refinish the woodheads. A few individuals stepped up to train and equip themselves to meet that demand, and custom clubmaking was reborn.

By the early 1980s, wooden woods and forged irons all but disappeared in the wake of the new metal woods and investment-cast cavity-back irons. Almost every advertisement carried promises of better performance, even if it meant tampering with club lofts and not telling you. But you already know about the "vanishing loft disease" phenomenon from Myth #1.

Almost overnight the demand for golf club refurbishment disappeared, and, it was thought, the modern clubmaker with it. But the clubmakers did not go quietly. They began to demand clubheads to go with the shafts and grips they were already buying. The result was that a cottage industry began to flourish.

The arrival of metal woods and cast irons meant none of the big golf club companies could manufacture their own clubheads. It was simply not cost effective for a golf club company to build its own casting foundry, so all golf companies bought their heads from subcontracted foundries. Thrilled to expand their production to include golf clubheads, the foundries realized they could also sell heads to a market of club repair people. This began what many refer to as the golf component industry, but that industry also quickly generated a dark side.

In order for any golf club to sell, there has to be a demand. To generate that demand, there has to a marketing campaign to convince golfers that they need or want the new clubs. To come up with the money for marketing, profits have to be high enough to pay the manufacturing bills and leave enough left over to buy ads and TV commercials, and to pay pros to endorse your clubs. If you don't have the money to generate a demand through advertising and endorsements, what can you do? Well, some people decided that the solution was to make cheaper-priced imitations of the clubs for which demand had already been generated. Thus began the dark side of the component industry, which you know today as "knock-off" clubs or "clones."

Unfortunately, professional clubmakers were blindsided by this turn of events. Golfers simply lumped everyone who could assemble a head, shaft, and grip into a golf club into one barrel of rotten apples. They assumed that anyone who made golf clubs from component parts was a knock-off artist who made cheap, poor-quality clubs. That discrimination (or I should say, lack of discrimination) is still with us.

Today, unfortunately, the legions of people who call themselves "clubmakers" are still split into two camps. On one hand are those who build cheap clubs that bear a resemblance to the heavily marketed standard made clubs; and on the other there are those who approach the craft in the same way a tailor crafts a suit to fit perfectly for a customer. In my book, those who make no effort to learn the art and skill of clubfitting—who simply glue a clubhead to a shaft and slide on a grip—have no place in this profession. On the other hand, those who study clubfitting technology and have a passion to build the best possible clubs for each golfer, one at a time, are without question the finest purveyors of golf clubs on the planet. So, how do you find the latter and avoid the former?

**Certification:** There are two professional organizations of custom clubmakers that offer accreditation exams for their members. The Professional Clubmakers Society (PCS) is one. PCS members who have achieved the Class A Clubmaker and/or Class A Clubfitter accreditations are truly among the best in this field.

The other organization, the Golf Clubmakers Association (GCA), is a for-profit division of a component company. The

GCA began to offer accreditation testing in the 1990s, and any clubmaker who has earned the GCA Advanced or GCA Professional accreditation most definitely knows his or her craft.[4]

The problem is that the vast majority of clubmakers are *not* members of either of these professional organizations, and have not taken any exams. In some cases this is because the clubmaker does not have the skills to qualify, but in other cases it's because … well … custom clubmakers tend to be a fiercely independent lot. There are any number of superb clubmakers who simply are not "joiners" and feel no need to prove to *anyone* through some exam that they know their stuff.

**Location:** Skilled clubmakers are in business to create for you the best possible clubs that the technology of clubfitting (and USGA rules) will allow. You will find some of them working in their own stand-alone, brick-and-mortar stores. You will find some of them working at golf courses and driving ranges. And you will find some of them working at home out of their garages and basements, doing their work as an avocation.

My point here is: *don't be put off by where you find them.* Some of the best clubmakers in the country work out of their garages and basements. Jerry Hoefling, Sr., the clubmaker chosen by the PCS as its 2004 Clubmaker of the Year, which means he is among the best of the best, works from a shop in his home in Saginaw, Michigan. So, where a clubmaker is working, or what city he or she is in, is no indication of whether they know what they're doing.

So, if certification is not an absolute indicator, and location is not an indicator at all, what's left?

What's left is you!

First, you have to *educate yourself* as to what constitutes a properly fitted golf club. Reading this book or any of my other ones is a good place to start. In fact, at the moment, it's the *only* place to start.

---

[4] The reason I know that these exams are good, by the way, is because I am the guy who wrote the original accreditation tests for both organizations, and I can tell you my goal was to make these tests truly identify who is good in the craft.

Second, you have to *ask around*. Talk to your friends who have been custom fitted. What did they like and not like about their clubs, their clubfitting, and their clubfitter? Talk to the pro at your golf course or driving range, or talk to a golf instructor. Ask if they know of any clubmakers in the area that they could recommend. As a last resort, look in the Yellow Pages. (I describe that as a "last resort" because many excellent clubmakers do not advertise in the Yellow Pages and rely solely on word of mouth.)

Another way of doing it is through the Internet. You can visit my web site, www.twgolftech.com, and look for the "Clubmaker Locator" link. The clubmakers I list are individuals I personally know and, in many cases, have personally taught. I can guarantee they are well schooled in accurate custom clubfitting.

Third, you have to *evaluate the clubmaker*. If you are looking to have a club or set of clubs fitted, reread Myth #25 (I was "custom fitted" …) before you visit the clubmaker. In fact, while you're at it, reread all four myths in that section (#25, #26, #27, and #28). Then, go talk to him or her. Describe what you want and ask about the process for making it happen. If what the clubmaker describes sounds pretty much like what I described as a "Level Four" fitting under Myth #25—then you've found a keeper.

The important point here is this.

*The best golf clubs you will ever own are those that have been properly fitted to your size, strength, athletic ability and swing characteristics.* Bar none. Remember what I told you about baseball bats and tennis rackets in the introduction to this book? Every other "stick-and-ball" sport commonly sells its "sticks" in all the custom fitting options its players need to play their best … except golf.

Yes, it might take a little more "product knowledge" on your part, and you might have to go through a bit of extra effort to find your clubmaker. But, believe me, the results will be worth every bit of it, and, as an added bonus, you'll probably pay no more (and very likely less) than you would have paid at the big box store.

# And Some Final Thoughts on the "Grass Ceiling"

Throughout this book I've perhaps been a bit harsh on some individuals and institutions. Targets have ranged from the retail golf industry, to club salespeople, to the major golf club corporations, golf magazines, and even the USGA itself. If you think I have gone over the line, I'm sorry if you were offended. It was not my intention to do that; after all, I've been a part of this industry my entire working life. I honestly believe some of these people mean well and that they really do love this game. Others … well, to be honest, I think the only reason they exist is to make money. Either way, it's time to look at things from a different perspective.

I believe the golf industry is currently killing the goose that laid the golden egg. As I pointed out in the introduction, each year about three million people leave the game of golf. Partly that's because golf is a difficult, often frustrating, game, but much of it has to do with the fact that the golf industry has foisted equipment on these golfers that *could not possibly* meet their needs. We have forced them to crash into a grass ceiling of our own making. For literally millions of golfers this has resulted in frustration, embarrassment and, eventually, departure from the game.

The golf industry's business model of making standard, mass-produced clubs to be sold off the rack in pro shops or retail golf stores began in the early 1900s. From that time through the 1970s, many of the specifications of their standard made clubs were far more beneficial for average golfers than are those resulting from the way the big golf club companies make their clubs today. Woods were much shorter, loft angles were higher, different face angles were available, and competition between the golf club companies was friendly. Even as recently as the late 1980s, no golf club company was larger than $70 million in annual revenues, and a new golf club model would remain on the rack for at least three years.

Today there are five golf club companies that now constitute more than 75 percent of the premium golf club market. Four of the five are publicly traded and are subjected quarterly to pressure from their stockholders and Wall Street financial analysts. Competition is far from friendly, and the new golf club model that debuts every March goes on closeout in October to make room for the next new "latest and greatest" solution to your shotmaking woes. Big-time marketing campaigns are the rule to get golfers stirred up, and companies that cannot afford $50 million a year to fund the campaigns find it tough to stay on the dance floor. That's why only five companies own the bulk of the premium golf club business while the other fifty all fight for the table scraps.

Competition among too few huge companies for golf club sales is what has caused today's drivers and woods to become too long, loft angles to become too low, and shot-correcting face angle options to disappear. To support these sales the industry's marketing focus has had to shift from straightforward honesty and more individual attention to each golfer, to promotion of the kind of myths that I am happily debunking for you in this book.

During the Tiger Woods boom of the 1990s, the golf industry could get away with just about anything. If the game lost three million players a year, it easily gained a similar number or more. But the bloom is off that rose. Today we are on the verge of losing more golfers than we're gaining. Golf equipment sales are flat to down; rounds played are flat to down; more golf courses are closing than opening; and that situation is not being helped by selling more 9-degree, 46-inch-long drivers to unsuspecting golfers who have never broken 100 in their lives.

So, where do we start? Here are some of the changes I think need to occur.

**Retail Stores**

- Retail stores need to work with local professional clubmakers to provide ongoing training to their sales staffs. These salespeople need to know almost as much about golf clubs as a knowledgeable clubmaker if they are to guide golfers toward the best choices for their game. And while we're at it, golfers are not well served by salespeople who have to choose between telling the truth and making a higher sales commission. You don't need golfers to start perceiving your stores as the factual equivalent of a used car lot.

- Every significant golf store needs to have paid professional clubmakers on its staff or at least on call. These would be people who are suitably trained and who can build true custom clubs, and where necessary properly retrofit the clubs people have previously bought or are currently buying. You wouldn't operate a clothing store without having at least access to a competent tailor. Why would you not do the same thing when you're selling even more expensive golf equipment?

## Major Club Companies

- The major golf club companies need to understand that ultimately their future will depend on selling clubs that meet the very real needs of very real golfers. If someone wants a 46-inch driver, fine, they can order it. But the golf industry needs to stop selling clubs that they surely *know* are wildly inappropriate for the average golfer, and then making it seem as though he or she is witnessing the second coming of sliced bread. Let me put it another way. The average golfer might not know much about golf clubs, but golfers assume *you,* the industry, do. They trust you. They think that you will not lead them astray. Don't betray that trust!

- The major club companies also need to give their designers responsibility for major input into, and possibly veto power over, marketing campaigns. Maybe, if that happens, we'll have less lunacy like systematically altering clubhead lofts so you can claim your clubs "hit farther," and ultimately you'll have more sales.

- Both the major club companies and the custom clubmaking supply companies need to start designing clubs that are specifically created to be of more direct use to the average golfer. For example, there ought to be many more models with high-lofted options, more clubs with significant offset, more significant hook-faces, etc., along with completely new and innovative approaches and designs. (In fact, you could start by shortening the darn drivers! Good Lord, you golf company people. What are you thinking?)

## The Golf Media

- The golf media need to play their part as well. Golf print and television media need to understand that they are as much the "guardians of the game" as major organizations like the USGA and PGA. They have a duty to report on golf equipment with the same journalistic integrity and skepticism as reporters in any other field. If calling a turkey a turkey frosts off some of your advertisers, so be it. You'll survive, so will they, and the game will be *far* better off. Let me repeat what I said to the club companies. The average golfer assumes that you know about golf clubs. They have placed their trust in you and your magazines or TV programs. They assume that you will give them an honest opinion—an opinion that is your best and most informed. *Don't betray that trust!*

- The golf media also need to vastly improve their role in golf education. No, I am not talking about doing yet another TV program or article on how to cure the slice. I am talking about educating the general golfing public as to how and why golf clubs work the way they do. No sport has a playing public that is, in general, as grossly uninformed about equipment as golf.

## Professional Clubmaking Associations

- The professional clubmaking associations have to understand that, by far, their number one task is to educate the golfing public about golf equipment. If growing the profession (and your organization) through consumer education isn't your overwhelming priority, what is? I mean, what are you doing that could possibly be more important than *that?* And, let's be honest—if you don't do it, who will?

- Perhaps a good place to start would be for these organizations to give clubmakers the tools (lesson plans, handouts, etc.) that they need in order to work with local retail stores and golfing groups. I would guess that more golf club misunderstanding comes out of those stores in one day than comes out of a professional clubmaker's shop in a year. You know that's happening, so why not work with the stores to help correct it? It might be good for *both* of your businesses.

## The USGA

- And finally, perhaps the USGA needs to realize that the gap between a PGA Tour pro and a weekend golfer is more than "one has more time to play golf than the other." *They are literally playing two different games.* Perhaps it's time for both the equipment rules and the game rules to reflect that reality—for the good of the game.

But if there is to be a "Grass Ceiling Revolution," the ultimate responsibility has to be on the shoulders of you—the person reading this book—the average golfer.

Earlier I pointed out that, as a golf consumer, you don't get what you pay for; you get what you *demand*. Okay, maybe there was a time when you were in the dark about what should be demanded, but you aren't now. As a result, the burden now shifts to *you*.

A number of years ago there was a movie called *Network*. In it the main character, a slightly deranged TV news anchor, urged everyone to go to their windows and yell: "I'm mad as hell, and I'm not going to take it anymore." They did, and their shouts spread from building to building, neighborhood to neighborhood, until the whole city was screaming the phrase.

I think something like that is what is now needed in golf. Indeed, in a way, I think it has already started.

Let me give you an example of how this could, and probably should, happen by relating a true story I received from a woman golfer who happened to read my book *The Search for the Perfect Golf Club*.

She wanted to get a new set of clubs and was leaning toward a particular well-advertised brand and model. But she also wanted to get clubs that were tuned to the way she plays. So, with my book in mind, she went shopping at one of the large retail golf chain stores.

I'll let her tell the story in her own words …

"Despite the fact that I am bigger, stronger, and more athletic than most women, it started just like you said. The salesman walked me right to their ladies' club department, pulled a driver off the rack, and handed it to me. He told me to get into my setup position and waggle it a few times. I did, and he immediately said that the club 'looked right' for me.

"I asked him whether the shaft length and flex were okay. He responded by telling me that the company that designed the clubs knew exactly what a woman golfer needed and all that was built into this driver.

"I mentioned that I was a little more athletic than most women golfers and asked about a men's model but with a senior flex. He took me over to the store's hitting net area, told me to hit two or three shots, and, again, announced that I was going to be fine with the women's club he first handed me.

"At that point I was getting more than a little mad, so I decided to take a different approach.

"When we went back over to the ladies' department to look at irons, right in the middle of his sales spiel, I made a motion with one of my fingers as if I was brushing something off my lip. This of course distracted the salesperson, who asked what I was doing. I told him that he had something on his lip. He asked what it was and I responded, 'I am not sure, but it must be from that total bullshit coming out of your mouth!'

"At that point, shocked though he was, I thanked him for his time, turned and walked out of the store, and went to find a custom clubmaker. A week later I had custom fitted clubs, built specifically for the way I swing and play, and I have been happier with those clubs than any other set I've ever owned. Thank you for writing the book."

Now you might wind up perhaps selecting more delicate language, but I think you get the idea of what needs to be done. It really *is* time for you, the average golfer, to finally stand up and say: "I'm mad as hell, and I'm not going to take it anymore."

Or, let me put it another way.

You can't expect a four-billion-dollar-a-year industry to change course unless you are willing to do at least *something* to help deflect it. If you love this game—I mean *really* love this game and want to see it handed down with its integrity intact to your children and grandchildren—then that is not too much to ask.

You could start by educating yourself more about golf equipment. Many of you already belong to a golfing group that meets on a regular basis. That might be a formal organization or simply a group of friends who play golf on a regular basis. Why not include an "equipment myths" educational component to it as a regular part of your visit to the "19th hole?" Why not invite a professional clubmaker to your golf or country club to discuss some of the myths I've mentioned in this book, or talk about some of the latest directions in golf club design or clubmaking? Why not hold some discussions based on this book or any similar ones?

At a minimum, every one of you, whether you belong to a formal golfing group or not, can do at least ONE of the following:

- The next time you go into a retail golf store, golf course, or driving range, ask if they have a professional clubmaker on staff, or on call.
- If you find retail salespeople who are not satisfactorily knowledgeable (having read this book, you'll be able to spot them in an instant), ask the storeowner or manager if he's seen the retail staff training recommendations in this section of the book.
- Write or e-mail the major golf magazines and/or other golf media and tell them that you want to see more equipment articles that provide a genuinely critical analysis of the equipment you are expected to buy.
- If you run into a professional golf clubmaker, ask what he or she has done to work with the local retail establishments, or the local golfers, to increase golf club literacy. While you're at it you might want to ask what their professional organizations have done along those lines.
- Write or e-mail the USGA and ask for the development of equipment rules and playing regulations that realistically

take into account the needs of the average player as well as the professional.

- Write or e-mail the major golf club companies and tell them that you really *would* like to know the technical specifications of their products (written so a layman can understand them), and you really would like to know the basis for their advertising claims. While you're at it, maybe you could ask why there are not more advances in equipment for the female and senior golfer—not to mention senior women golfers.

I could go on listing more, but these will give you the general flavor. I'll leave it to your creativity to devise others.

I believe the golf industry has gotten so wrapped up in playing its billion-dollar games that they have completely forgotten the person who makes this industry possible—the average, get-in-a-round-when-I-can, shoot-in-the-90s-on-a-good-day golfer. But it is that same golfer who can and I believe will provide the needed course correction.

If the golf industry continues to ignore him—*and her*—it does so not just at its own peril, but at the peril of the greatest game ever invented. And *that* would be the greatest tragedy of all.

# About the Authors

**Tom Wishon** has been a leading golf club designer for more than thirty-three years. He is among an elite group of designers whose clubheads have won tournaments on the PGA Tour, the Champions Tour, and the Ryder Cup. In all, Wishon has more than fifty design "firsts" to his credit. He has few peers in the fields of clubhead design, shaft design, and clubfitting research.

In addition to his design work, he has written eight books on golf clubmaking and design, including the best-selling *The Search for the Perfect Golf Club* and *The Search for the Perfect Driver*—both of which won Book of the Year honors from the International Network of Golf, a nonprofit association of golf media professionals. Wishon has written more than two hundred magazine articles on clubmaking technology and has been on the *Golf Digest* technical advisory panel for more than ten years. He also serves as the technical advisor to the PGA of America's website.

**Tom Grundner** is a retired college professor who, as a second career, started his own full-time custom club business and eventually became a Golfworks master golf clubmaker. Now retired (a second time) he lives in Tucson, Arizona, where he indulges his loves of building handcrafted custom putters and writing books about the eighteenth-century Royal Navy.